PENGUIN BOOKS

I Don't Know What I Want, But I Know It's Not This

Julie Jansen has made five career changes within the broadcasting, contingency recruiting, outplacement, and training industries in order to find work that fulfills and satisfies her professional and personal needs. Currently, she coaches and consults to individuals and companies, helping them to be successful in their work. Jansen has been featured in publications such as the *WSJ.com Career Journal, Selling Power, Working Woman, Information Week, Motivated to Sell,* and *Smart Money,* and has been published in the *National Business Employment Weekly.* A frequent speaker for associations, nonprofit groups, and corporations throughout the United States, she lives in Stamford, Connecticut.

I Don't Know What I Want, But I Know It's Not This

—

A Step-by-Step Guide to Finding Gratifying Work

JULIE JANSEN

Penguin Books

PENGUIN BOOKS

Published by the Penguin Group

Penguin Putnam Inc., 375 Hudson Street,
New York, New York 10014, U.S.A.
Penguin Books Ltd, 80 Strand,
London WC2R 0RL, England
Penguin Books Australia Ltd, 250 Camberwell Road, Camberwell,
Victoria 3124, Australia
Penguin Books Canada Ltd, 10 Alcorn Avenue,
Toronto, Ontario, Canada M4V 3B2
Penguin Books India (P) Ltd, 11 Community Centre, Panchsheel Park,
New Delhi-110 017, India
Penguin Books (N.Z.) Ltd, Cnr Rosedale and Airborne Roads, Albany,
Auckland, New Zealand
Penguin Books (South Africa) (Pty) Ltd, 24 Sturdee Avenue,
Rosebank, Johannesburg 2196, South Africa

Penguin Books Ltd, Registered Offices:
Harmondsworth, Middlesex, England

First published in Penguin Books 2003

5   7   9   10   8   6

Copyright © Julie Jansen, 2003
All rights reserved

LIBRARY OF CONGRESS CATALOGING IN PUBLICATION DATA
Jansen, Julie.
I don't know what I want, but I know it's not this : a step-by-step guide
to finding gratifying work / Julie Jansen.
p.   cm.
Includes bibliographical references and index.
ISBN 0-14-200248-8
1. Career changes. 2. Job satisfaction. 3. Career development. I. Title.

HF5384 .J36 2003
650.14—dc21   2002028991

PRINTED IN THE UNITED STATES OF AMERICA
Set in Garamond 3 with Bodega Serif Light
Designed by Susan Hood

To my brother Dave. I wish you were here.

Acknowledgments

I would like to express my heartfelt appreciation to the following individuals:

Lucy Hedrick, without whom this book would not exist, who encouraged me and coached me in her inimitable no-nonsense style *and* introduced me to my agent, Denise.

Thanks to Denise Marcil, my wonderful agent who believed in me from minute one and really engaged in this project, turning it into a reality.

Jane von Mehren, my gifted publisher, a consummate professional and an amazing editor, whose gracious style is much appreciated.

Jessica Kipp, who is such an insightful, diplomatic, and patient editor.

Ben, my honey, who believes in me no matter what.

Lora Friedman, who stuck with me through thick and thin during the first stage of this project and whose talent and friendship were instrumental to my success.

Diana Carter, whom I relied on for her enthusiasm, humor, ideas, and close friendship.

Acknowledgments

Chris Beggs, my lifelong dear, dear friend, without whom my life would not be what it is. Thanks also for spoiling me with spectacular flowers every step of the way.

My dad, who drove me to the public library every Saturday of my childhood so that I could read, without which I might never have discovered my passion for the written word.

Melody, who so completely contradicts the "wicked step-mother" myth and is a blessing in my life.

Zeke, who kept me company day and night when I was writing, and whom I miss so.

Momster, who is such a treasure and my words soulmate.

Joy Baldridge, who is a constant joy and role model for me.

Robert Montello, who never ceases to be an unfailing source of support for me.

Bonnie Depp, who grounded me and provided sanity when it was much needed.

Sheila Goldman and Rober Miller, for sharing my excitement in Nantucket.

Mark Rubinfeld, you always were sure I would write.

Kim and Chris, I love you.

All my friends and acquaintances who shared their stories with me.

My extended family of close friends and business colleagues for supporting and believing in me along the way.

Contents

Contents

Introduction

There are so many people who aren't happy, fulfilled, or even moderately satisfied with their work. In fact, while I was writing this book, and someone would ask me what it was about, I'd explain that it was about how to find satisfying work for the rest of your life. Without exception, that person would say either "Boy, I sure could use your book right now!" or "My husband [neighbor/sister/son/cousin] desperately needs your book."

This has never discouraged me because I know exactly what someone who is unhappy needs to do to find gratifying work. Work has given me much more than just an income. It has provided me with stimulation, freedom, challenge, independence, and emotional fulfillment. It has also given me the opportunity to make a difference to others.

I started working when I was eight years old. I bought candy at the drugstore and sold it to my classmates at a significant markup. My formative years were spent working at a variety of jobs—cutting lawns, switchboard operator, selling plastic pools and fertilizer, cashier, bartender, bookkeeper, and even impersonating the Easter bunny.

I graduated from college with a degree in mass communications, and became a research analyst for a television station, then a copywriter for radio. After my brief stint in broadcasting, my next three careers included recruiting, outplacement, and training. In hindsight, these career choices seemed accidental and unrelated, but each one of them focused on people and work, my two strongest interests.

I am now in my fifth career, as a speaker, consultant, and career coach, which has made me even more intrigued by how and why people choose the work they do. I wrote this book to motivate others—to help them feel confident that being happy with work is a choice you *can* and *should* make. I empathize with those of you who are not happy or satisfied and have had difficult work experiences. Why? I've had many myself. I have been fired, my job has been eliminated, I have had nasty bosses (two), and I have been caught in mergers and political battles. I have also worked for companies whose corporate cultures were a bad fit for my needs and I even had an ex-employer threaten to sue me because I had signed a noncompete clause. I have been bored, disinterested, unchallenged, and miserable as well as stimulated, engaged and fulfilled. What did I learn through all of these experiences? Discovering the right work for you *will* give you the motivation and confidence while building a strong foundation, which will enable you to bounce back, and renew or even reinvent yourself when you need to do it.

I Don't Know What I Want, But I Know It's Not This

—

PART I

Where Are You Now?

—

CHAPTER 1

Why Do You Want or Need to Change Your Work?

"I'm turning forty this year and all of a sudden I'm questioning what I'm doing workwise. I've never had these feelings before. It's crazy!" says Kim, senior vice president of human resources at one of the largest banks in the United States.

Maybe you can identify with Kim's comment and her feelings of confusion about work. The workplace of today and what is predicted for the future certainly doesn't resemble the workplace that most people entered ten, fifteen, or thirty years ago. For a variety of reasons, it has become increasingly difficult for most of us to feel satisfied with our work situation. Louise Lague, a psychotherapist and author, sums it up well: "Technology has made it possible to work all the time from anywhere. This has made many workplaces hell on earth—they never close! Deadlines are tighter, more is expected, and weekends and evenings are consistently interrupted."

The constant changes taking place in companies, including the temporary nature of jobs that were once relatively permanent, create a stressful work environment in which people find it difficult to feel satisfied, let alone happy. Seemingly endless communication (e-mail, voice mail, meetings), multiple projects with multiple deadlines and extreme pressure to increase profits, all contribute to an atmosphere in which many workers feel overwhelmed.

Debbie sold nurse-call systems to hospitals for a giant health-care solutions company. She felt so much stress from nonstop travel and unrealistic sales goals that she finally quit, taking a job that didn't have the same upside potential financially, but also one that wouldn't be nearly as stressful. After giving notice at her former company, she spoke with ten or more individuals at various levels in the corporate hierarchy to say good-bye. She was shocked when every one of them told her that she was lucky to be able to quit, and if they felt they could leave their jobs, they would do so immediately. They made comments such as: "It's not what it used to be" and "The company doesn't support us anymore; all they care about is profits."

"Burnout is not caused by too much work," Louise Lague explains, "but by working all day on projects that have no meaning to you personally. It takes much more psychic energy to do something you hate than something you love." When you are working at a job that you dislike, these negative feelings take over all of your free time, including weekends. Lague continues, "It's entirely likely that projects that once excited us no longer do. We live and grow and keep learning and when healthy people stop learning, they get bored and yearn to learn something new. It's a mistake to think that there's something wrong with job dissatisfaction—it's absolutely normal and healthy."

Kim, the human resources executive mentioned earlier, works for a bank that recently acquired two large companies—the eighth acquisition in three years. The greatest problem posed by these acquisitions is the inability of the organization to successfully merge the disparate corporate cultures. This organizational stumbling block has resulted in higher employee turnover and confusion about shared values and goals. Not only has Kim been affected personally, but, as a senior human resources executive, she also must deal with the serious repercussions the mergers have on other employees.

Even though people know intellectually that hard work and loyalty aren't important to most employers in the way they once were, it is difficult for most of us to accept it on an emotional level. The opportunities for advancement that once existed have decreased significantly as well, causing confusion about what to strive for in one's job. This is especially true for the more seasoned worker, who in the past was always motivated by working toward his or her next step up the organizational ladder.

Many people are also feeling the stress brought on by multiple generations working together. In their book *Generations at Work,* for example, Ron Zemke, Claire Raines, and Bob Filipczak describe the disconnect between baby boomers and Gen Xers: "Boomers see Xers as alternately greedy and lazy, suspicious and self-serving, loners and cynics," and "Xers, for their part, see Boomers as obsessive, 'my way or the highway,' a little naïve, a little soft." The negative perceptions that each generation has of the other lead to conflict, frustration, and distrust—not the optimal ingredients for a comfortable work environment.

Many people over the age of forty are feeling increasingly dissatisfied because they are experiencing either subtle or blatant discrimination from their employers. Joanie, at fifty-two, has sold advertising time in television for her entire career. When she was fifty years old, her boss stripped her of her national sales manager title and responsibilities, telling her, "You're fifty now and shouldn't be traveling as much." Many people in their forties and fifties believe that businesses are more interested in the young and technologically savvy worker. In particular, people who were laid off in their late forties and fifties are, in many instances, convinced that their age had a lot to do with the decision. People in this age range believe that companies, especially large corporations, perceive workers older than forty-five as less creative, less flexible, and more expensive than younger employees.

And, indeed, there is ample evidence that older employees are often replaced by young people who are willing to work like crazy. When these younger workers become managers, it can and often does lead to discomfort or outright conflict with older employees who once held these same jobs. The bottom line? Older employees often don't want to stay with companies where they are perceived in a negative light simply because of their age.

———

Yet another reason employees feel frustrated and dissatisfied is that most corporations, whether large or small, still manage their employees based on the old "bricks-and-mortar" model in which "everyone works in one place." Many companies either can't figure out how to design a new model or are changing very slowly to support different lifestyle needs and create a flexible workforce. People get frustrated with this slow pace and increasingly are going to work for savvy companies who they think meet their employees' needs in this area. Ben, for example, designed audio equipment for a small company, commuting 112 miles every day for three years. Even though he could be very productive working in his home office, his employer didn't believe in telecommuting, thinking that if an employee wasn't in his company office, he wasn't working. Although Ben loved his job, his boss, and the company overall, at forty-seven, he wanted to eliminate, or at least reduce, the stress of a long commute. He found a job with a larger audio company and now works from his home. When he gave his notice to his employer, in an attempt to keep him, they grudgingly agreed to allow Ben to work at home once a week. While it was tempting to stay, Ben knew they never would fully support him and he accepted the new job. As he anticipated, he feels healthier and the stress created by driving a long distance to work every day is gone.

In today's work climate, more and more individuals are beginning to question the grueling pace at which they lead their lives. In an effort to manage this issue, some companies have instituted policies that support maintaining "balance" between work and an employee's personal life. For example, several years ago, Microsoft created a new vacation policy for its senior executives that allows them to take as much vacation as needed. Although research shows that most high-level executives don't use all of their allotted vacation time, this was Microsoft's way of showing appreciation for its leaders. In fact, a survey conducted by Personnel Decisions International, a human resources consulting company, in 2000, revealed that nearly half of the workers surveyed at all levels said that the time they commit to work has increased in the past five years, with the average workweek for a full-time employee clocking in at 49.2 hours. And according to a Families and Work Institute study, 16 percent of those surveyed bring work home more than once a week. Verizon, a major telecommunications company, surveyed its employees about working while on vacation, and half admitted they either call in to work or check their e-mail while away on vacation. What does all this prove?

Psychologically, the concept of introducing balance into one's life seems far-fetched and unrealistic for many workers. Why? The demands of today's workplace are excessive for most people. With technology allowing twenty-four-hour communication, employees feel obligated to work all the time, whether it be on weekends or on vacation. Even more important, many companies that have policies that support balance can give employees a mixed message about whether it's acceptable to leave the office at a reasonable hour or take all of the vacation and personal time allotted in the company employee handbook. If senior management and the corporate culture demonstrate that succeeding means working around the clock, then the pressure of fitting in and "doing what it takes to get the job done" can override the desire to lead a balanced life.

In most cases, the challenge of creating a more balanced work life does not mean stopping work. Regardless of age, many of us feel that our sense of self is wrapped up in our work, and psychologically it would be difficult to stop working altogether, even if we could afford to do so financially. The financial need to work is primary for most people. In *Age Works,* Beverly Goldberg explains that when Social Security legislation was enacted in the mid-1930s, the average life expectancy was a bit less than sixty-two years of age, with individuals older than sixty-five comprising only 7 percent of the population. By contrast, in 2000, 13 percent of the U.S. population was older than sixty-five, with that percentage continuing to increase.

A multitude of financial implications flow from these statistics. People rely on Social Security, pensions, and personal savings to finance retirement. Many people are not confident, however, that Social Security as we know it today will continue to exist in the future. As for pension plans, Goldberg notes that more than half of Americans who are employed by companies are not covered by an employer-provided retirement plan. The most revealing statistic, from a survey conducted in the late 1990s by the Employee Benefit Research Institute, is that 35 percent of people in their forties and early fifties were not very confident about their ability to maintain a comfortable lifestyle after retirement.

In addition, baby boomers, who comprise the largest segment of the working population, are notorious for their poor saving habits. According to Ken Feltman, executive director of the Employers Council on Flexible Compensation, of all the generations, boomers have the largest credit card debt and an average of twenty years remaining on their mortgages. Because of this, many of us will find ourselves working longer and retiring later than previous generations.

People are also dissatisfied for a number of reasons that don't necessarily have to do with the company they work for, or the workplace overall. Instead, they have found themselves, either gradually or suddenly, feeling discontented or disenchanted with their work. Such feelings have more to do with the individuals themselves than with how they feel about their employer, and may stem either from inner conflicts or from a longing for something different.

It is no longer true that the majority of people who question whether their values and goals are being met are middle-aged. Although many events that typically occur in midlife—such as the death of a parent or a child leaving for college—may cause us to think more clearly about what is important to us, there is no age limit on searching for happiness and fulfillment in work and life. The failure of the many "dot com" companies in the late 1990s caused many people in their twenties and thirties to examine what they needed and wanted next from work.

Although many employees are unhappy in their work, some of these people probably don't even know *why* they are unhappy, yet they acutely feel the symptoms of their discontent. These feelings can range from being depressed, bored, lethargic, and apathetic to being overwhelmed, stressed, or unchallenged. Those who do understand the reasons for their dissatisfaction are usually stuck; they find it easier to remain in an unhappy work situation than to learn how to "unstick" themselves.

Work in the twenty-first century is dramatically different from the way it was in the 1960s, 1970s, 1980s, and early to mid-1990s. Engaging in a single career or lifelong trade is no longer the way we work or will work in the future. Instead, the demands of the marketplace as well as our personal lifestyle choices dictate the kind of work we do and the way we structure it. Because of this, the capacity to shift gears more easily where work is concerned has become a critical skill for those intent on achieving a significant measure of life satisfaction. Learning to master this ability and make it your own will alleviate much of the discomfort and pain that you may have experienced in the past, or may be feeling now.

Living is about making choices. Deciding what kind of work will make you happy is a choice, a big one. Today, there are so many choices that sometimes it may seem easier to sit still and not make any at all. But you have a clear choice—you can either decide to begin the process of change, or you can continue doing something that isn't making you happy.

This book is about learning how to identify and create work that is right for you. The odds are that once you've read this book and have decided that you are ready and committed to change your work, you will look for a new job or career, and possibly leave the kind of work you've been doing for many years. Whatever you decide to do, there is one important point to bear in mind: work is not "one size fits all." Your ability to make smart choices about the kind of work you do depends very much upon who you are as an individual.

Every person I work with as a career coach feels unhappy or unfulfilled in his or her work or career. These people often tell me that many of their colleagues feel the same way but are resigned to their situation or are not sure how to change it—so they don't. It's not abnormal or wrong to feel dissatisfied with work; but if you are feeling consistently negative about it, it is a mistake *not* to make changes in your work.

Now it's time to move ahead and begin your journey toward a life of satisfying work!

CHAPTER 2

What Is Your Work Situation?

There are six work situations that represent a specific contemporary work-life challenge that you may be facing right now. Reading about these work situations will enable you to label and isolate the reasons for your desire to change your work and, in doing so, gain a clearer understanding about how to alleviate your dissatisfaction or discontent. While you probably will relate to one of the six work situations more than the others, it is highly likely that you will identify with two or three of them. They are:

1. *Where's the Meaning?* These individuals are looking for a new kind of reward and satisfaction. They may be seeking personal fulfillment or be driven by a strong desire to help others in need. Bill, for example, was an engineer for fifteen years, but never really enjoyed his work. After being downsized by his company, a telephone equipment reconditioning business, Bill took some time off, volunteering for five different organizations. He currently earns money by working several part-time jobs. His wife volunteers for many of the same organizations, and Bill tells me that they are both happier and having more

fun than they ever had when they were earning substantially more money.

2. *Been There, Done That, but Still Need to Earn.* These people have been, and continue to be, successful in their work. They want, and probably need, to keep earning at the same level, yet can't conceive of staying in the same job for another ten or twenty years. Many of these individuals won't be able to change careers immediately, but with planning can do so eventually. A prime example is Melinda, who has worked as a computer systems programmer for most of her career. She stayed where she was for a while because she was making good money and financial responsibilities precluded her from changing. As her children started growing older, she began to work as a personal fitness trainer at night and on weekends. Once Melinda's life situation changed (her children grew up and she divorced her husband), she was able to launch full-time into her personal training business with established clients. Today, she is making very close to the same amount of money doing something she actually enjoys.

3. *Bruised and Gun-shy.* These individuals are victims of the changing workplace. Having been laid off or discriminated against, they are hesitant to either join the corporate world again or take any kind of career risk, and yet they do need to continue working. Juan, after having been laid off, had a quadruple bypass during the transition period and decided to become what he calls a "job stress coach." Ambivalent about reentering the corporate world, he now has his own practice helping others deal with the stress of working.

4. *Bored and Plateaued.* Many people have worked hard for many years and are simply ready to make a change because they are bored and are looking for new challenges. Deborah, at age forty, had spent her entire career in consumer-products marketing. A vice president at an elite marketing firm, Deborah admitted that she was "bored to tears." She remembered the early years of her career as being exciting and fun. For at least four

years, however, she had felt stagnant and finally became so miserable she decided to actively seek a new direction.

5. *Yearning to Be on Your Own.* These people dream of being on their own or starting a company. According to Helen Harkness, author of *Don't Stop the Career Clock,* in the early nineteenth century, 80 percent of Americans were self-employed. By 1970, this number had fallen to 9 percent. But today self-employment is growing at a furious pace; in 2000, there were 12 million small businesses. By 2020, it is predicted that 25 percent of businesses will be small, privately owned companies. Another different type of self-employment is the "contingency workforce"—people who work temporarily on specific projects for many different companies—which has grown by 57 percent since 1980. These workers don't have many of the responsibilities that a business owner has, yet they possess the flexibility that people experience in their own businesses. Some contingency workers receive benefits and some may not. With the increased stress of working for a company, more and more people are realizing that working on their own can satisfy their specific needs. After spending thirty successful years in teaching, sales, and human resources, Blanche started her own consulting firm several years ago. She says, "I always knew I wanted my own business and to have my stamp on something." She is having a lot of fun, and hitting every goal she sets for herself and her business.

6. *One Toe in the Retirement Pool.* These people are often baby boomers who want to semiretire or retire from their current work. What they do with the years ahead is a question that many boomers are asking themselves—do they change careers completely, volunteer, scale down the time they are working in their current job, or just retire completely? Di retired when she was fifty-eight from a long career in sales because her exhausting travel schedule was affecting her health seriously. The first few years of her retirement, she took yoga, read books, and learned how to paint in oils. Recently, she has started doing

some training seminars for a previous employer, and is enjoying the combination of retirement and part-time work.

Take a few moments and look at the descriptions of the six situations. The following list of questions will help you to identify your primary work situation, as well as the others that you fit within, and will provide you with additional clarity about why you associate with a specific circumstance. Taking this assessment may confirm what you already suspect about your reasons for being discontented with your work and allow you to gain further insights.

What Is Your Work Situation?

Read each question carefully and answer yes or no as quickly and as easily as you can. The questions are grouped by work situation, and while you may think you fit only into one or two categories, you should answer all the questions to get a complete picture of your own circumstance.

WHERE'S THE MEANING?

1. In the last year or so, have you ever asked yourself, "Why am I doing the work I'm doing?" Or "What is the point of the work I do?"

    N   (Yes)   No

2. I'm not exactly sure what doing meaningful work means to me, but I'd be interested in finding out.

    N   (Yes)   No

3. It is important that I directly touch or make a contribution to others as often as possible in my work.

    N   Yes   (No)

4. I am feeling more and more that there is no reward or challenge for doing the work that I do.

    Y   (Yes)   No

5. I fantasize about "throwing in the towel" and going to work for a nonprofit organization or a specific cause.

Yes   No

6. There are several charities or special causes that I am very interested in learning more about, and perhaps getting involved in, even simply as a volunteer.

Yes   No

7. My family and friends don't believe that I am making a difference in the world with my work.

Yes   No

8. I've experienced a traumatic or sad event in the recent past that has caused me to think about what is really important to me as a person in both my work and life.

Yes   No

9. I have an interest or hobby that I am passionate about and that I wish I could become more deeply involved with.

Yes   No

10. At one time, it was important to me to meet my financial and achievement goals in my work, but this doesn't seem to matter to me anymore.

Yes   No

BEEN THERE, DONE THAT, BUT STILL NEED TO EARN

1. My work is no longer providing me with opportunities to do what matters to me, yet I'm used to my income.

Yes   No

2. I feel as if I have achieved a lot in my current career and would love to try a different kind of work but am afraid that I wouldn't earn what I do now if I did try something else.

Yes   No

3. Earning the same amount of money or more is important to me so that I can take care of my family, but I am a little bored.

 (Yes) No

4. I really enjoy my work but feel as if I've had every possible experience in my career. Despite this, I honestly can't see changing careers because it would probably mean earning less money.

(Yes) No

5. I have a lot of financial responsibilities that cause me to feel insecure about changing careers and earning less money.

Yes (No)

6. While money is a big reason that I am afraid to change my work, if I think about it, I can find a realistic way to reduce or even eliminate my expenses in the next year or two.

(Yes) No

7. I'll admit that I've been pretty bored and unchallenged in my job lately, but I'm hard-pressed to think of anything else I could do and earn the same paycheck.

(Yes) No

BRUISED AND GUN-SHY

1. I've had a tough job experience that caused me to lose my job or derail my career for a period of time and find it's still hard to describe my experience or even think about it without feeling angry, upset, or having other negative emotions.

Yes (No)

2. I don't feel optimistic about the future of my career, in part because of my past negative work experiences.

Yes (No)

3. I have been fired at least once. I still feel a little bitter about my experience, and though I'm not thrilled with my work sit-

uation, I can't seem to think about making a change for fear it could happen again.

Yes (No)

4. I am unemployed and can't seem to find the energy to focus on finding work that I enjoy, let alone a job of any kind.

Yes (No)

5. I don't trust the corporate world anymore. When I started working, company loyalty was important. Joining a company meant you stayed there forever.

Yes (No)

6. I've experienced some hard knocks in my career. I've been laid off, gotten caught in company politics, been discriminated against, or my company has been sold. How much more do I have to take?

(Yes) No

7. It seems that what companies want from their employees keeps changing. I just don't know if I can keep up this pace any longer, but I can't afford to stop working either.

(Yes) No

8. I've thought about becoming self-employed or changing careers, but I've been so burned that I'm afraid to make any changes.

Yes (No)

BORED AND PLATEAUED

1. I've been working in the same job for more than two years without a change in responsibilities and can perform my tasks effortlessly without stretching myself.

Yes (No)

2. I've invested a lot of time and energy in my work and am considered an expert in my field, yet I feel the need to change something about it, however minor that change may be.

Yes (No)

3. I am so busy with tasks and projects that I don't have time to "smell the roses."

(Yes)   No

4. I have been having trouble getting out of bed in the morning, especially during the week, and feel unmotivated when I'm at work.

(Yes)   No

5. I daydream about quitting my job and doing something entirely different because I don't feel passionate about my work anymore.

(Yes)   No

6. I am experiencing feelings of burnout (anger, frustration, depression, and anxiety) at work.

(Yes)   No

7. I guess after so many years in my field, I should think about doing something different. But what would I do?

(Yes)   No

8. Although I know that my peers respect me, I'm starting to wonder if people think that I have any passion for my job anymore. In fact, I have been wondering that about myself.

(Yes)   No

9. I moved from another firm a few years ago in my industry in hopes that I would feel reinvigorated. I am starting to feel the same way I did before I changed jobs—stale and unstimulated.

(Yes)   No

10. I've just begun to notice that I am not being included in important meetings regarding policy or strategy as much as I used to be. I'm feeling as if I'm not contributing anything new, either.

Yes   (No)

11. Meetings, employees, and clients are all starting to look the same. This feeling scares me, but I'm not sure what to do about it.

Yes   No

YEARNING TO BE ON YOUR OWN

1. I no longer feel fulfilled by working for someone else and just don't think another job will give me what I'm missing now.

Yes   No

2. I am increasingly dissatisfied with the way the company I work for is run, and I'm convinced that I can do things differently and better.

Yes   No

3. I grew up in an entrepreneurial family or am close to someone who is an entrepreneur. I can see the advantages of having my own business—more than I fear the disadvantages.

Yes   No

4. I'm so envious of people in their own businesses. I know it's not easy, but the thought of being my own boss is so appealing.

Yes   No

5. I've always dreamed of being in my own little business. I know there are plenty of resources out there for entrepreneurs, but I am not sure where or how to begin.

Yes   No

6. I know that being on my own doesn't have to mean starting a company. I would like to learn more about my options for self-employment because it's very attractive to me.

Yes   No

7. I know I want to go into business for myself someday but have never been a good salesperson. I'm afraid that not being comfortable with selling will cause me to fail.

Yes   No

8. I've thought a lot about the kind of work I'd like to do next, and I'm convinced that being an entrepreneur is my next move.

Yes   No

9. The idea of being an independent contractor or "free agent" is incredibly appealing.

Yes   No

10. I'm very independent and have always had trouble with politics and working on teams. I am beginning to think that some form of being on my own makes sense for me.

Yes   No

ONE TOE IN THE RETIREMENT POOL

1. The truth is, I really would like to stop working right now. It just seems unrealistic to do so financially.

Yes   No

2. I never want to stop working completely, but I would like to slow my pace down a bit and do something different and less demanding.

Yes   No

3. I've been obsessing more and more about not working and spending more time with my family and with my hobbies and interests.

Yes   No

4. I'm stressed out from the demands of working and my health isn't what it should be. I'm seriously thinking about retirement.

Yes   No

5. I'm worn out from working. I've thought about my alternatives, and partial retirement seems like the best one for me as long as I can work part-time.

Yes   No

6. I've worked for a long time and would welcome ideas about structuring the next phase of my life.

Yes   No

SCORE KEY

Check below the categories in which you answered yes to four or more of the questions. Those are the work situations that describe how you are feeling about work right now.

☐ Where's the Meaning?
☒ Been There, Done That, but Still Need to Earn
☐ Bruised and Gun-shy
☒ Bored and Plateaued
☒ Yearning to Be on Your Own
☐ One Toe in the Retirement Pool

Now it's time to move forward and learn more about yourself, your preferences, needs, and desires—for your work and for your life. Once you've done this by completing the self-assessments in chapters 3 and 4, you may choose to move through this book either sequentially, or in a zigzag fashion. Each work situation is discussed in its own chapter with case studies of people who fall into the particular situation.

You will learn a three-step process for leaving your current work situation behind, and moving toward something new or different, or merely changing aspects of your work to create what's missing.

Step 1: Complete the Self-Assessments Specific to Your Work Situation

The first logical step to putting a plan together for your career is to learn and understand what your unique values, interests, personality preferences, attitudes, and favorite skills are. By using this information about yourself as a foundation, you'll be better able to focus your job search or career direction. Each of the six work situations requires additional assessments specific to your circumstance and the direction you'd like your career to take.

Step 2: Explore Roadblocks and Opportunities

Many obstacles and barriers may be preventing you from pursuing a different kind of occupation or changing the way you work—for example: age, money, time, education, and a lack of experience. On the positive side, the opportunities are limitless. In this step, you will learn how to get around roadblocks and exploit your opportunities.

Step 3: Create an Action Plan

An action plan requires quite a bit of thoughtfulness and preparation. While creating your plan requires a lot of time and energy, it is an extremely valuable tool to use for mapping out a new career or revamping your career goals.

———

Although the journey that this book will take you on is not easy, it should be fascinating and eminently worthwhile. Ultimately, it will bring you to your desired destination—satisfying and fulfilling work for as long as you'd like to do it.

PART II

Where Do You Want to Be?

CHAPTER 3

Values, Attitudes, and Change Readiness

Whether you merely want to tweak your work situation or change it dramatically, it is essential that you get to know the one person who will be indispensable to your quest for work that fits—*you.* Understanding who you are—your values, attitudes, preferences, and personality traits—is the key to discovering the kind of work that will bring you personal fulfillment. Here's a simple analogy: If you invite friends over for a home-cooked dinner, you need to know exactly what ingredients to use in preparing the meal. When you throw in just any old ingredients, your guests will leave hungry and disappointed because the food you cooked tasted awful. Your values, personality traits, attitudes, and abilities are all like the ingredients of a recipe. Without knowing what they are, you will find it difficult to use these ingredients to help you create nourishing work.

A common mistake that many people make after deciding they are unhappy in their work is to jump immediately into updating their résumé and answering help-wanted ads on the Internet or in the newspaper and completely overlook the first and very necessary step—self-assessment. According to psychologist Suzanne Roff, director of Compass Point Consulting,

LLC, a firm that specializes in career and organizational assessments, "With so many people dissatisfied with the work they do, it's more important than ever to think about job fit. Career assessments help begin an exploration process. There is no one direction for an individual, but some directions are just more viable than others. It often takes gathering more information and getting some help to make an advantageous change."

Bottom line? Don't skip this chapter or chapter 4! Read them, complete the assessments, and refer back to them as you read the rest of the book. In addition to helping you create your ideal work situation, the self-assessment process can help you uncover a whole new repertoire of words, phrases, and concepts that will add a rich new dimension to your résumé and job interviews. Not only will this make you feel more confident and prepared, it will also have a positive effect on the people who meet you.

Assessment: What Is It and How Is It Used?

"Assessment" is a generic term used to describe the various tests, questionnaires, quizzes, surveys, inventories, and checklists used by career counselors, job search consultants, outplacement specialists, coaches, and other career management professionals to assist their clients. Using self-assessments will allow you to collect and evaluate your own preferences, experiences, values, needs, skills, and other personal traits. It is a foundation to help you identify or create the most suitable possible work opportunities for yourself. In other words, self-assessments help you find work that fits. Just imagine how productive the world would be if everyone who works found work that truly suited them.

The assessments in this chapter fall into three categories:

- Values
- Attitudes
- Change readiness

Some people are fearful or intimidated by the assessment process because of what they may learn about themselves. Let's be perfectly clear: the assessments in this book are not psychological or clinical tests. In no way can a conclusion about your sanity or any personality dysfunction be ascertained from your answers. Self-assessments simply reaffirm what you already know about yourself—whether consciously or not—and provide you with a framework within which to pursue your quest for more satisfying work.

Joan has worked for several years in the search business for an agency recruiting and placing marketing professionals, and has never been happier in her work. Before this, she worked as a senior administrative support professional. She truly believes that if she hadn't taken several self-assessment tests after being laid off from her last administrative position, she wouldn't be working in recruiting today. By completing the self-assessment process, she was able to decide on a different direction for herself, one that she would never have considered otherwise. "Each person has a distinct personality and specific abilities which need to be guided toward possible career paths that are suitable for them. When someone's decisions are based on these assessments, there will be a higher degree of success in a particular occupation; therefore, the result is greater fulfillment and happiness because they are doing what they were meant to do in life. I'm living proof of this!" Joan says.

Let's begin your self-assessment process.

Values

A value is defined as a principle, standard, or quality considered inherently worthwhile or desirable. Individuals, groups, and whole societies hold values. Values are what motivate and fulfill you. They imbue your work and your life with meaning. Values either can be personal and non-work-related or completely work-related. In most cases, however, the values that are important to you will inform both your work life and your personal life. In essence, a value is what is important to you. While career psychologists have identified well over one hundred possible values, the list you are about to read contains forty values.

In this assessment, you will first identify all the values that are important to you. You will then narrow down the list to your ten most important values. Last, you'll identify which of your top-ten values are satisfied in your current work situation. This process will help you understand what's missing now so that you can be clear about what you're not willing to be without in the new work you choose.

Read the following list and place a check mark in the box to the left of each value that is important to you. Check as many as you'd like. Be careful not to check a value that you think "should" be of importance to you. Check only those you truly live by, or are committed to living by in the future. For now, ignore the boxes on the right of each value.

List of Values

☐ Achievement/accomplishment: producing results that are significant; completing tasks and projects successfully. ☐

☐ Advancement: consistently moving ahead to new and progressive opportunities. ☐

☐ Autonomy: ability to choose own projects, set own pace, schedule, and work habits, minimal supervision of your efforts. ☐

☐ Balance: spending equivalent time and effort on tasks, work, and overall life. ☐

☐ Belonging to a group: having a sense of being a contributing member of a group. ☐

☐ Building something: creating or establishing a thing or idea. ☐

☐ Challenge: involvement with stimulating or demanding tasks or projects. ☐

□ Competition: engaging in activities where results are measured frequently and compared with others'. □

□ Creativity: making, inventing, or producing innovative, imaginative, or original things or ideas. □

□ Doing good: contributing to the betterment of the world. □

□ Entrepreneurship: organizing, managing, or starting a business or enterprise. □

□ Equality: having the same capability, quantity, effect, value, or status as others. □

□ Excitement: involvement with new and dynamic experiences with variety and change, perhaps risk. □

□ Fame: possessing extreme visibility, a great reputation, being recognized and renowned. □

□ Family happiness: focusing on relationships, time spent with and attention given to children, spouse, parents, or relatives. □

□ Financial security: pay and benefits that are satisfactory and predictable. □

□ Friendships: frequent and caring relationships; camaraderie and interaction with others. □

□ Fun: experiencing pleasure, amusement, and enjoyment. □

□ Happiness: feeling or showing pleasure and satisfaction, contentment and well-being, joy or cheerfulness. □

□ Harmony: feeling inner calm and tranquillity. □

□ Health: optimal functioning of body, mind, and spirit. □

□ Helping others: giving assistance, support, and aid to others. □

□ Independence: self-reliance; freedom from the influence, guidance, or control of others. □

□ Integrity: strict personal honesty; firm adherence to a moral code. □

□ Leadership: guiding, motivating, or directing others. □

□ Learning: acquiring knowledge and satisfying curiosity. □

□ Leisure: pursuing non-work-related activities. □

□ Personal development: challenging your capabilities; acquiring new skills and demonstrating abilities. □

☐ Physical activity: involvement in activities that rely on your body and physical exertion. ☐

☐ Recognition: being positively acknowledged by others; being given special notice or attention. ☐

☐ Respect: being treated with consideration and fairness. ☐

☐ Risk-taking: facing unknown or dangerous challenges or demands. ☐

☐ Safety: freedom from danger, risk, or injury. ☐

☐ Security: protection from fear, anxiety, or danger; a guarantee of the fulfillment of an agreement; predictability. ☐

☐ Self-expression: ability to communicate personal ideas, emotions, or feelings. ☐

☐ Spirituality: participating in a religious or ecclesiastical belief system. ☐

☐ Stability: maintaining an enduring, dependable, and predictable situation. ☐

☐ Status: possessing a prestigious position or rank. ☐

☐ Teamwork: working closely with others toward common goals; having close working relationships. ☐

☐ Wealth: owning a significant quantity of money or possessions. ☐

If there are values that are important to you that are not on the list above, write them down in the blank lines below.

☐ _____ ☐

☐ _____ ☐

☐ _____ ☐

Now that you've selected all of the values that are important to you, you'll narrow down the list to your top-ten values. Read through your selections on the preceding list of values and check the box to the right of any value that you absolutely cannot, or will not, live without. Ask yourself, "When I've been the happiest in my life, was this value fulfilled? Is this truly *my* value or is it an unrealistic or inauthentic ideal that I really don't live by?" If you are unable to identify ten values, that's fine. However, do try to limit your number to a maximum of ten. In the spaces below, write down your ten values in any order.

VALUE	YES	NO
1.	☐	☐
2.	☐	☐
3.	☐	☐
4.	☐	☐
5.	☐	☐
6.	☐	☐
7.	☐	☐
8.	☐	☐
9.	☐	☐
10.	☐	☐

Next, think about your current work situation. To the right of each value, check yes or no to indicate whether or not this value is being expressed in any aspect of your work right now. When you are pursuing a different kind of work, or simply trying to change the dynamics of your current career, it is very important to know which values are most significant to you.

———

Mary has a strong need for financial security and stability. These two values are fulfilled for her in her current job as an analyst for an investment bank. Two of her other values, however, are respect and balance, neither of which is being satisfied for her right now. Mary works with colleagues who are demanding and rude, and she consistently works sixty to seventy hours a week along with a three-hour daily commute. Mary really enjoys the kind of work she is doing and intends to look for a similar job in an industry other than investment banking. She plans on being very careful this time about assessing the culture of prospective employers to ascertain how employees work together and the ways that the company values its employees' time by supporting flextime, telecommuting, vacation, and reasonable deadlines.

By working for a company that does not support respect and balance, Mary learned about which values are truly important to her the hard way. If Mary had known that respect and balance were so important to her, she would have asked probing questions during her interview in an attempt to understand the work environment.

You have the benefit of learning what your primary values are now so that as you move through the process of changing your work, you can keep your top-ten list of values foremost in your mind. Continually refer to your list when you are analyzing and thinking about different work options.

Attitudes

Attitude is your state of mind or feelings with regard to a person, idea, or thing. Research has consistently shown that one's attitude directly motivates one's behavior. In a positive sense, those who possess an optimistic attitude about a goal or challenge are far better equipped to overcome any barriers to achieving that goal. On the other hand, an individual who has a negative attitude will find it much more difficult to achieve his or her goal. The process of assessing yourself and your work can be nerve-racking if you allow it to be. Self-assessment requires time, honesty, patience, and introspection. But even if you are willing to put in the time and effort, your overall attitude can "make or break" your ability to reach your goals.

This simple assessment focuses on your attitudes toward yourself and toward the external world as they pertain to work. For each statement, circle the word that most closely describes how often you feel or act that way.

1. I have enough confidence in myself and my abilities that I am willing to take reasonable chances and do things I haven't done before in order to create satisfying work for myself.

Almost never   Seldom   Sometimes   Frequently   Almost always

2. I am uncomfortable promoting myself and think that if I'm doing a good job, the right people will notice.

Almost never   Seldom   Sometimes   Frequently   Almost always

3. I find that I really know the things I'm good at and not good at, and think that self-evaluation is for people who are less experienced.

Not at all   Seldom   Sometimes   Frequently   Almost always

4. I feel that I put the maximum amount of time, energy, and enthusiasm into my work that I'm capable of doing.

Almost never   Seldom   Sometimes   Frequently   Almost always

5. I feel that relationships are very important to my career success and have developed and maintained strong relationships with people both within and outside my company and industry.

Almost never   Seldom   Sometimes   Frequently   Almost always

6. I initiate contact with my boss, my clients, and my subordinates consistently, offering support, feedback, and appreciation whenever possible.

Almost never   Seldom   Sometimes   Frequently   Almost always

7. Given the rapid pace of change and excessive demands of employers and clients today, I don't believe that true job satisfaction is possible anymore.

Not at all   Seldom   Somewhat   Frequently   Almost always

8. When I have learned something new or make a meaningful contribution to my organization or industry, I document it immediately and then celebrate my success.

Almost never   Seldom   Sometimes   Frequently   Almost always

9. I set short-term goals for myself and include action items, which I take very seriously.

Almost never   Seldom   Sometimes   Frequently   Almost always

10. I am clear about my career goals, realizing how important it is to have specific goals, monitor my own performance, and get myself back on track if I need to.

Almost never   Seldom   Sometimes   Frequently   Almost always

11. My job is so demanding that I am simply unable to get involved with professional development or keep up with reading the trade publications in my industry.

Almost never   Seldom   Sometimes   Frequently   Almost always

12. I work at keeping up-to-date on trends and other information about industries besides my own.

Almost never   Seldom   Sometimes   Frequently   Almost always

SCORE KEY

For each statement, match your answer with the numerical value listed below. For example, if you answered Seldom for statement 1, your score is 2. Then add your scores as directed below.

1. *Almost never* *Seldom* *Sometimes* *Frequently* *Almost always*
   1   2   3   4   5

2. *Almost never* *Seldom* *Sometimes* *Frequently* *Almost always*
   5   4   3   2   1

3. *Not at all*   *Seldom* *Sometimes* *Frequently* *Almost always*
   5   4   3   2   1

4. *Almost never* *Seldom* *Sometimes* *Frequently* *Almost always*
   1   2   3   4   5

5. *Almost never* *Seldom* *Sometimes* *Frequently* *Almost always*
   1   2   3   4   5

6. *Almost never* *Seldom* *Sometimes* *Frequently* *Almost always*
   1   2   3   4   5

7. *Not at all*   *Seldom* *Somewhat*   *Frequently* *Almost always*
   5   4   3   2   1

8. *Almost never* *Seldom* *Sometimes* *Frequently* *Almost always*
   1   2   3   4   5

9. *Almost never* *Seldom* *Sometimes* *Frequently* *Almost always*
   1   2   3   4   5

10. *Almost never* *Seldom* *Sometimes* *Frequently* *Almost always*
    1   2   3   4   5

11. *Almost never* *Seldom* *Sometimes* *Frequently* *Almost always*
    5   4   3   2   1

12. *Almost never* *Seldom* *Sometimes* *Frequently* *Almost always*
    1   2   3   4   5

SCORE KEY

Add the total of scores for questions 1 and 2.
_____ This is your score for Self-confidence.

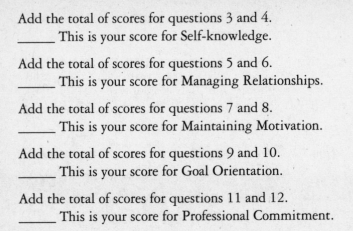

Add the total of scores for questions 3 and 4.
_____ This is your score for Self-knowledge.

Add the total of scores for questions 5 and 6.
_____ This is your score for Managing Relationships.

Add the total of scores for questions 7 and 8.
_____ This is your score for Maintaining Motivation.

Add the total of scores for questions 9 and 10.
_____ This is your score for Goal Orientation.

Add the total of scores for questions 11 and 12.
_____ This is your score for Professional Commitment.

WHAT DO YOUR SCORES MEAN?
Self-confidence

If your score for self-confidence is 6 or below, you may be feeling as if you have no value in your work, or you are not appreciated by your employer. It may be that you are not taking any risks in your work, or are not feeling optimistic and open. It is more difficult to make changes when your self-confidence is not healthy. Exploring and dealing with your reasons for lower self-confidence is important. Has something happened to you in the recent past that has caused your self-confidence to erode? Can you focus on achieving something that will improve your self-confidence?

Self-knowledge

If your score is 6 or below in this category, your assessment of yourself may not be as accurate as it could be. Honestly evaluating your strengths as well as the areas in which you may need more development, and asking others for feedback, may be useful exercises for you to undertake. If you are unrealistic about how well you really know yourself, then you will have difficulty identifying the best possible fit for yourself in relation to work.

Managing Relationships

A score of 6 or below in this category could indicate that you don't value relationships with others, or that you have concerns about your effectiveness in dealing with other people. Networking is a crucial part of learning about the external world, and without strong relationships to help you, the process of exploration can be painful.

Maintaining Motivation

If you have scored 6 or below in this category, it is possible that you have neglected your career. Staying focused and energized is up to you. If you aren't consistently thinking of ways to maintain your focus and energy where your career is concerned, you will have difficulty feeling motivated. This, in turn, will make it more difficult to achieve your goals.

Goal Orientation

If your score falls below 6 here, you probably don't have a focused plan of action toward achieving specific outcomes. Setting reasonable yet challenging goals and really believing in them will help you keep motivated, especially when you want to do something different with your career.

Professional Commitment

It is likely that you are bored with your work or career if you scored below 6 in this category. Think about the reasons you entered your present line of work. What about it energizes you now, or has in the past? Your answer to this question may help you regain some of your sense of commitment to your profession. On the other hand, if you have difficulty coming up with a satisfactory answer, it may make sense for you to begin the process of changing the type of work you do.

If your work situation is less than desirable, your score may be low in one or several of these categories. Don't be overly concerned! Instead, sit up and think about why this is so and what you can do about it. Any of these areas can be developed with motivation, guidance, and the right tools.

———

Richard has been a photographer for twenty years, and has grown increasingly unhappy with the way the photography business has changed. He isn't getting enough photo shoots to pay for his studio and support his family and realizes that he probably will have to close his business. Unfortunately, Richard's self-confidence has eroded so badly that he feels paralyzed about pursuing another career. In addition, he thinks that because he isn't good at networking or managing relationships, he won't be successful at uncovering new job opportunities. He isn't motivated to find a job and certainly doesn't have any kind of plan in place to move forward. Richard really needs to focus on each of these areas before he can move ahead in finding new work.

Your attitude as reflected by these six categories is something to be aware of as you think about changing your work. When you are happy and satisfied with your work, your score in each area will be very high.

Change Readiness

Most people don't like change. For many of us, change can be difficult or uncomfortable. This is true regardless of whether the change is forced upon us, planned, unexpected, or self-created. Why? Because we are giving up familiarity in exchange for the unfamiliar and unknown. When this occurs, we experience a myriad of emotions, including frustration, uncertainty, and fear. *Who Moved My Cheese?* by Spencer Johnson, M.D., is a simple ninety-four-page parable offering a quick, easy, and fun way to understand change and deal with it quickly and effectively. Fear of change and what it represents is one of the reasons that people don't reevaluate their work. This assessment on change readiness is intended to help you increase your self-awareness about your comfort level with change. If you understand more clearly what your threshold of tolerance is for change, it will be easier for you to handle change and even make it happen. This is an important thing for you to know about yourself, because change is an unavoidable part of learning to find gratifying work.

When answering the following questions, indicate how each statement is true for you by placing the appropriate number in the blank to the left of the statement.

5 = *Definitely true*
4 = *Often true*
3 = *Somewhat true*
2 = *Scarcely true*
1 = *Almost never true*

___1___ 1. I can honestly describe myself as someone who seeks out change regularly.

___3___ 2. I'm rarely surprised by changes at work because I usually see early warning signs and can prepare myself in advance.

___2___ 3. I am constantly trying to learn new skills even when there isn't an immediate need to do so in my job.

___1___ 4. When there is a change initiative going on within my company or with my clients, I am often asked by leadership to become involved in the process and implementation early on.

___3___ 5. I find it easy to look at a business problem from a different standpoint even if I haven't taken this approach in the past.

___3___ 6. When an employee or colleague suggests another way of handling something, I encourage him or her to try it even if someone else has already tried it this way in the past.

_2_ 7. I work very hard at staying current in my field by belonging to professional organizations, networking with people outside my company, and keeping up-to-date with trade publications.

_1_ 8. I look forward to changing my work or career with great excitement.

SCORE KEY

Add up the numbers that you entered for each question. If you scored:

8 to 19 points	You have significant difficulty dealing with change. Change is simply not comfortable for you and you tend to avoid it at almost all costs.
20 to 29 points	Although you are able to handle change under the right circumstances, you have to be highly motivated to instigate it.
30 to 40 points	Your ability to anticipate and handle change is admirable. You are usually adept at creating and responding to change.

Anyone can learn to deal more effectively with change if there are real reasons to do so and a reward for changing. If you are unhappy with your work situation, instigating and accepting change is very important if you are to find satisfaction in your work.

CHAPTER 4

Personality Preferences, Interests, and Favorite Skills

Now it's time to learn about who you are and what makes you unique, based on your individual characteristics and your personality, interests, and skills. The self-assessments in this chapter fall into three categories:

- Personality preferences
- Interests
- Favorite skills

Personality Preferences

Personality is the totality of an individual's distinctive traits. Although aspects of your personality can change slightly as a result of experience and self-awareness as you move through your life, your inherent personality was developed by the time you were two years old. You cannot change the essence of who you are, but you *can* change your behavior. When you are looking for a good fit between who you are and the kind of work you do, it's important to know what your personality preferences are so that you can ensure that they will mesh with your work.

Your personality encompasses many traits. The following quiz assesses some of the traits that have proved to be important when considering a career. There are no right or wrong answers when taking a personality preference test; however, it is important to respond quickly and intuitively. The questions may seem very black and white in nature, but this is intentional.

1. I like people for the most part; however, I prefer to work on my own.

Yes   No

2. When I enter a roomful of people I don't know, I feel shy and uncomfortable.

Yes   No

3. When I frequently have to deal with people on the phone and face-to-face, I feel drained by the end of the day.

Yes   No

4. I'm often thinking about what "could be" instead of what exists now.

Yes   No

5. New ideas, insights, and inferences really excite me.

Yes   No

6. I get bored very easily with projects that I'm working on.

Yes   No

7. I do not believe that it's very important to follow rules, regulations, and guidelines as closely as possible.

Yes   No

8. When involved in a business deal or transaction, my first concern is how the other person feels.

Yes   No

9. I'm more likely to be described by others as "enthusiastic and warm" rather than "calm and cool."

Yes   No

10. When someone at work asks me to stop what I'm doing to help him or her with a project, I feel disjointed.

Yes   No

11. I love schedules, definite deadlines, and planning.

Yes   No

12. I like having all the information before I begin a project and get uncomfortable when priorities change.

Yes   No

13. I am not afraid to speak up if I believe in something, even if everyone else disagrees with me.

Yes   No

14. I prefer to be the leader rather than have others lead.

Yes   No

15. I try very hard to get people to see my way of thinking.

Yes   No

SCORE KEY

Write down the number of times you answered yes for the following sets of questions:

Questions 1 to 3	2
Questions 4 to 6	2
Questions 7 to 9	2
Questions 10 to 12	1
Questions 13 to 15	2

WHAT DO YOUR SCORES MEAN?
Introverted or Outgoing

If you answered yes more often for questions 1 to 3, you tend to be more introverted. You enjoy your solitude, don't like being the center of attention, and typically work out problems and ideas by yourself.

If more of your answers are no, you are more outgoing and prefer to be with people more often than not. You probably have many social relationships and are expressive and easy to read.

Idealist or Realist

If you answered yes more often to questions 4 to 6, you prefer to imagine possibilities and are more of an idealist. This means that you love new ideas, insights, and inferences and tend to focus your energy on the future and what could be instead of what exists now.

If you answered no more often for questions 4 to 6, your focus tends to be more on reality and less on possibilities. You take things more literally, preferring the specific and realistic rather than what you can't see or have to imagine.

Emotional or Factual

Answering yes more often to questions 7 to 9 indicates that you are more emotional than factual. Being emotional means you tend to be more focused on feelings and your personal values.

If your answers are more often no, you prefer to be factual, veering toward analysis, laws, rules, and policies.

Structure or Spontaneity

If your answers are more often yes for questions 10 to 12, you like structure and prefer planning with fixed goals that have definite deadlines.

If your answers were mostly no for questions 10 to 12, you are spontaneous and prefer goals that are more open-ended. You tend to be flexible and adaptable to changing situations.

Assertive or Acquiescent

Answering yes more often to questions 13 to 15 means your personality preference is to be assertive. This means you tend to be more dominant and more of a go-getter.

If you answered no to two or more of questions 13 to 15, you are more acquiescent, tending to have a more passive nature and preferring to be behind the scenes, rather than leading the pack.

How to Use This Information

Even if you are using skills in your work that you enjoy and are interested in the work you are doing, if your personality doesn't match your work you will not be satisfied. Kelly is an example. She is introverted, and a realist. She is emotional, acquiescent, and prefers structure. She works as a help desk professional and, while she enjoys the information technology field, Kelly goes home at night feeling exhausted by the constant barrage of phone calls and e-mails. She never seems to be able to accomplish what she sets out to do because she is constantly interrupted by requests for help from the employees of her company. Because she tends to acquiesce rather than lead, she isn't able to take control of her situation.

After you've taken the personality test, write down your preferences and compare them to your work environment to see if they fit. Let's see how Kelly's list looks:

PERSONALITY PREFERENCES	KELLY'S WORK ENVIRONMENT
Introverted	Deals with people constantly.
Realist	Kelly solves computer problems by collecting all the facts first, even if it takes a long time.
Emotional	Kelly's boss and many of her colleagues focus on following rules and policies when making decisions.

Structure	There is a process that the employees of Kelly's company are supposed to follow when they need help, but this rarely happens.
Acquiescent	Kelly's passivity allows her colleagues to be demanding of her. She constantly feels pushed into a corner, often agreeing to deadlines that are unrealistic because she feels uncomfortable setting limits.

Clearly, Kelly is working in a job that is not a fit for her personality preferences. Kelly would be much happier in an information technology role in which she interacts with people in a more structured way and can stick to a schedule that is self-imposed rather than forced on her.

Now you try:

_____

_____

_____

_____

_____

_____

_____

_____

If you've completed your comparison of your personality preferences with your current work environment, and you have discovered, as Kelly has, that there isn't a strong match between the two, this could be a very good reason for your unhappiness in your work.

Interests

An interest is something that you are willing to give special attention to because you either feel strongly about the subject matter or you like the way it makes you feel when you are engaged with it. The degree to which you feel passionate about your interests can vary dramatically, depending on your preferences with regard to the various topics or activities involved.

There are two steps to this first exercise. First, without thinking too intently, list ten activities or topics that interest you the most. They can be either work- or non-work-related. Don't worry if you can't come up with ten.

Next, remembering your values and personality preferences, under the heading "How It Makes Me Feel," write down two or three words or phrases to the right of each interest that describe how that particular interest makes you feel or why it arouses a willingness on your part to involve yourself with it. Let me use myself as an example.

INTEREST	HOW IT MAKES ME FEEL
1. Reading	Reading allows me to escape to another place or time. I get involved with interesting characters and I always learn something.
2. Speaking to audiences	Giving talks is a vehicle for expressing myself, using language, and helping people to learn and understand ideas and information. Speaking provides immediate recognition.
3. Watching movies	The visual involvement with stories and characters makes me feel entertained and engaged.
4. Organizing space or things	Appeals to my need for orderliness and makes me feel in control.

5. *Socializing one-on-one*	I get energy from people, and I'm very curious about others. It feels good to laugh, tell stories, and exchange information.
6. *Walking or sitting at the beach*	The beautiful environment and the sun relaxes me.
7. *Eating and drinking in restaurants*	A social activity, and I love the sensaations involved.
8. *Writing*	Venue for using language and helping others.
9. *Giving advice and solving problems.*	I like the intellectual challenge; I can make a difference.
10. *Riding on trains*	I like this speedy and efficient way to travel, and I find it relaxing.

Now you try:

INTEREST	HOW IT MAKES ME FEEL
1.	
2.	
3.	
4.	
5.	
6.	
7.	
8.	
9.	
10.	

Determining your primary interests is usually relatively easy; especially if you regularly spend time doing things like playing golf or making stained-glass windows. What is difficult for most people is thinking about interests in relation to work. Many people tend to separate the two because they believe that they won't be able to fulfill their interests through work. Yet, the people who are the most satisfied with their careers have found a way to tie their personal interests more closely to their work. This can mean creating more time outside of work to pursue their interests, or working in a field or industry that involves their interests. Here are two examples: Barry works as a sales manager in the grass-seed business. A major part of his job is playing golf—a sport that Barry is passionate about—with his clients, who are owners and managers of golf courses. Candace works in human resources, but her schedule is flexible enough that she can take two to three bike trips every year.

This assessment can help you think about how to relate your strongest interests to work. For example, I am a professional speaker, a writer, a coach, and a consultant. My work satisfies my interest in speaking to audiences, writing, giving advice and solving problems, and socializing one-on-one. I have often fantasized, however, about writing restaurant or movie reviews, which would combine my interests in writing, socializing one-on-one, watching movies, and eating and drinking in restaurants. Just because I love eating in restaurants does not mean that I want to own one or work in one. In fact, I have worked in restaurants and disliked it.

Can you think of ways in which you can tie your interests into work based upon the examples that have been provided? What are they?

_____

_____

_____

_____

_____

The next exercise is designed to help you understand your interest in specific types of work tasks and activities. Simply check the tasks and activities that appeal to you, regardless of the level of interest you may have. You may or may not have tried these tasks before. For now, ignore the letter that follows each item.

____ Scheduling tasks or meetings   (D)
____ Counseling someone   (P)
____ Chopping wood outside   (O)
____ Participating on a sports team   (P)
____ Operating machinery   (O)
____ Planting flowers or a garden   (O)
____ Learning new software   (O)
____ Keeping records   (D)
____ Preparing food   (O)
____ Taking care of someone who is ill   (P)
____ Analyzing and managing investments (D)
____ Negotiating a deal between two parties (P)
____ Writing a business or sales proposal   (I)
____ Conducting research   (D)
____ Revamping a compensation plan   (D)
____ Handling customer complaints   (P)
____ Going on a sales call   (P)
____ Designing an audio system   (I)
____ Word-processing a document   (D)
____ Organizing a desk   (I)
____ Teaching a class   (P)
____ Selling products in a store   (P)
____ Writing an article   (I)
____ Designing a Web site   (I)
____ Driving an eighteen-wheeler truck   (O)

____ Taking care of children (P)

____ Breeding racehorses (O)

____ Preparing financial statements (D)

____ Finding markets for new products (I)

____ Interviewing a job applicant (P)

____ Coordinating an event (I)

____ Writing a press release (I)

____ Repairing a watch (O)

____ Planning a budget (D)

____ Rewiring a house (O)

____ Building a cabinet (O)

____ Preparing accounting reports (D)

____ Finding a new office space (D)

____ Facilitating a meeting (P)

____ Acting as a travel guide (P)

____ Designing a costume (I)

____ Opening new accounts for customers (P)

____ Reviewing restaurants (I)

____ Managing a group of employees (P)

____ Raising money for a cause (P)

____ Creating spreadsheets (D)

____ Drawing maps (O)

____ Fighting a fire (O)

____ Analyzing census data (D)

____ Writing a book (I)

____ Reupholstering a couch (O)

____ Decorating a house (I)

____ Raising cattle (O)

____ Designing a new business procedure (D)

____ Conceptualizing a company vision (I)

____ Creating a marketing campaign (I)

____ Maintaining golf course greens (O)

____ Analyzing insurance risk (D)

____ Editing manuscripts (I)

____ Reviewing legal contracts (D)

Each of the tasks and activities listed above falls into a specific type of interest category. The four categories are People, Ideas, Data, and Objects. Now look at the letter in parentheses next to each task or activity. Count the number of P's, I's, D's, and O's you have, writing that number in the corresponding space below.

P _____
I _____
D _____
O _____

Read the definition of each interest category below. The category with the highest number is your dominant interest.

People
You enjoy activities or tasks that involve a lot of interaction with people, whether individually or in groups. You may enjoy persuading, teaching, coaching, counseling, or directing people. Regardless, the key for you in your interests is to be involved with people the majority of your work time.

Ideas
This category involves theory, concepts, creating or expression of feelings, philosophy, or beliefs. You probably tend to lean toward the arts, music, drawing, painting, sewing, and writing.

Data
You are most interested in concrete and realistic tasks that involve schedules, numbers, financials, directions, procedures, and processes. You appreciate and are comfortable with the finite and practical nature of tasks or activities that fall into this category.

Objects
You like working with your hands, repairing things, and the precise and orderly use of machinery, tools, and inanimate ob-

jects. Working with plants and animals are part of this category.

Most people are primarily interested in one of these categories, yet enjoy and want to be involved with tasks in another category as well. Bernie, for example, loves his work in technical sales, yet has a degree in engineering and really gets involved in the design and installation of the equipment he sells. He's fortunate enough to be able to satisfy his interests in two distinctly different areas.

Favorite Skills

A skill is an ability or expertise. A favorite skill is a skill that you not only possess but are also *interested in* and *willing to use.* This is the difference between a skill and a favorite skill.

Although a skill can be defined as a broad category, like verbal reasoning or spatial relations, this assessment is focused on helping you understand how to identify specific skills that you can and want to use in your work, such as writing or scheduling, for example. We all have skills that we are good at but that we are not necessarily interested in using frequently, or at all. While it is unrealistic to expect that you can avoid using certain skills without exception, it is not unreasonable to expect to spend the majority of your time at work using the abilities that you enjoy and are eager to use—your favorite skills.

For each skill or competency on the following list, you will assess two things:

1. What you believe your degree of proficiency is.
2. Whether or not you enjoy using it.

For degree of proficiency, use the scale provided and write the number that applies in the space to the right of the skill. For enjoyment, check those skills or competencies you enjoy using most in the space at the left. If you come across a particular skill that you haven't used in the past but think you'd enjoy using in the future, put an asterisk in the space at the left.

DEGREE OF PROFICIENCY

    0—*Untested/never tried*
    1—*Very limited*
    2—*Below average*
    3—*Average*
    4—*Above average*
    5—*Outstanding/mastery*

ENJOY MOST	DEGREE OF EXPERTISE
____ Writing business documents	____
____ Editing materials	____
____ Interviewing/hiring people	____
____ Mediating differences between people	____
____ Mentoring others	____
____ Negotiating deals	____
____ Public speaking	____
____ Facilitating a meeting	____
____ Presenting ideas	____
____ Coaching someone	____
____ Counseling someone	____
____ Teaching a class	____
____ Motivating people	____
____ Building a team	____
____ Leading a team	____
____ Training people	____
____ Helping others	____
____ Cataloging items	____
____ Handling scheduling	____
____ Keeping records	____
____ Conducting research	____

____ Evaluating ideas

____ Taking inventory

____ Setting standards

____ Assessing quality

____ Gathering data

____ Giving advice

____ Approving decisions

____ Delegating tasks/responsibility

____ Developing procedures

____ Managing people

____ Solving problems

____ Managing projects

____ Instigating change

____ Interpreting policy

____ Managing tasks

____ Analyzing budgets

____ Overseeing a profit-and-loss statement

____ Planning a budget

____ Cost accounting

____ Analyzing investments

____ Financial planning

____ Auditing

____ Developing policies

____ Conceptualizing new ideas

____ Developing strategy

____ Selling a product or service

____ Telemarketing

____ Creating a marketing plan

____ Writing proposals

____ Setting fee schedules

____ Creating an advertising campaign

____ Promoting a product or service

____ Coordinating events

____ Analyzing markets

____ Managing sales

___ Fund-raising   _____
___ Serving customers   _____
___ Handling customer complaints   _____
___ Working with computers   _____
___ Designing technical products   _____
___ Building something   _____

Now, from your list above, write down the ten favorite skills that you would most enjoy incorporating in your work (not necessarily in order of preference).

1.

2.

3.

4.

5.

6.

7.

8.

9.

10.

How many of your top-ten favorite skills do you use in your current job? Which ones?

_____

_____

_____

_____

How many are above-average or better strengths of yours?

_____

_____

_____

_____

Which ones could you develop more?

_____

_____

_____

_____

Which ones haven't you tried before?

_____

_____

_____

_____

Getting to know yourself as well as you can is always an enlightening and useful process. In some instances, your scores and results will merely confirm what you already know about yourself. In other cases, you may feel surprised by what you learn. Sometimes taking assessments will highlight ideas, assumptions, feelings, and strengths that you are aware of on some level but have not thought about in a long while or have kept submerged within your subconscious.

By going through the assessment process, you've taken an important and practical first step toward giving yourself insight into what kind of work will satisfy you. This, in turn, will help you devise an action plan and, ultimately, a solution for finding satisfying work. You will need to refer to your answers to all of the self-assessments as you create action plans for your specific work situation.

Now you will move on to the chapters that describe the six categories you read about in chapter 2. Each chapter will provide you with a description of the specific situation, stories of people who fit into the category, and additional assessments that you can take to help you identify what to do next. Your challenge will be to discover what you can do to find, create, or change your current work to meet your needs. Once you have identified these things and are able to couple them with the confidence to make the adjustments that are needed, the process will be easier and more fun.

PART III

How Do You Get There?

—

CHAPTER 5

Where's the Meaning?

In a survey that I conducted of 110 people, more than 90 percent ranked "finding meaning" as the number-one reason that
they recently had changed or would like to change their careers.
The concept of "finding meaning" has so many interpretations
that entire books have been written on the subject. The dictionary defines meaning as something that is signified, or that has
intent or purpose. To find meaning in work can denote being
passionate about what you do and whom you do it for, or it can
simply reflect your ability to set priorities in your work to satisfy your unique needs and desires. You may already know what
meaning is for you, and you may realize that it doesn't exist in
your work right now. Or you may not know exactly what meaning is for you, yet you know instinctively that it doesn't exist in
your current work situation.

Despite being aware of the absence of meaning in their lives,
some people never feel compelled to search for it. When it
comes to work, it is much easier to focus on earning a paycheck
to feed, clothe, and provide shelter for yourself and your family
than it is to examine your purpose and passion.

Every person is different; what is deeply meaningful to you may not matter to someone else in the least. The point is, to find meaning in your work, you first must know what matters to you.

Take the case of Steve, a financial consultant who owns his own business. Steve strongly believes that anyone can acquire financial security if they know how to plan their finances. He gets tremendous satisfaction every day from helping his clients learn how to handle financial challenges. Steve's top values are autonomy, family happiness, financial security, and helping others.

For Chris, a twenty-four-year-old administrative assistant at a television network, meaning comes from the knowledge that he is valued by his boss and coworkers for doing a good job. Even though the tasks he performs are essentially viewed as "grunt" work, he knows that he is needed. Chris is motivated by teamwork, recognition, respect, and learning.

Both Steve and Chris know what is meaningful to them. Based on the knowledge of what would bring a sense of meaning to his work, Steve, who had a previous career in sales, made the decision to get the necessary licenses and certifications so that he could help others manage their money. Chris knows that he won't be doing entry-level administrative work forever, and his mature attitude has enabled him to satisfy his need for meaning for the moment.

Whether you know what meaning is for you and realize that you don't have it, or don't know exactly what it is but feel as if you don't have it, one thing is certain. In order for you to find meaning, you need to be able to question the nature and purpose of the work you are doing now.

Step 1: Complete the "Where's the Meaning?" Self-Assessment

Before you learn how to incorporate meaning into your work, it is important to come up with your own personal definition of "meaning."

Your values are particularly important to understanding what meaning is to you. Remember that values are what fulfill you and motivate you. Go back to the list of values that you identified as most important to you on page 31 and review them.

Next, keeping your top-ten values in mind, ask yourself the following questions, and write down your answers.

1. When you think about the things you find meaningful, what comes to mind? Include things that are significant or important in your career as well as in your personal life. Your list of "things" should include ideals and feelings as well as activities.

   _____

   _____

   _____

   _____

   _____

2. Which of these things are you involved with now? Which have you done in the past? Which would you like to be involved with in the future? Be as specific as possible.

   Past

   _____

   _____

   _____

   _____

   Now

   _____

   _____

_____

_____

Future

_____

_____

_____

_____

3. Take another look at your answers to questions 1 and 2 and hone down your list. Be honest. Are there things on your list that you believe are meaningful but you know, deep down, you'd never really pursue?

_____

_____

_____

_____

It is very important to find out what is actually meaningful for *you*. Understand that for one person meaning may be about spending more time with her children by shortening her commute and working from home one day a week, while for another it could mean reading to the visually impaired. Also, be aware that the word "meaning" can be misconstrued to represent exalted ideals. In other words, meaning does not necessarily indicate that you are helping others or working for a charity.

Do not move on in this chapter if you are not clear about what meaning is for you. It is essential to know what you are working toward as you create a plan or learn how to overcome the obstacles to bringing meaning into your work.

One more point about knowing what is meaningful for you: Whatever you identify as having meaning for you today probably wasn't what was meaningful to you ten years ago, and may not be so twenty years from now. What is relevant about the process of identifying and finding your meaning is that once you learn how to do it, the next time will be that much easier.

Now, read the ten types of meaning and check the ones that are most important to you. You may feel that all of the ten types of meaning are important to you. If so, put an asterisk by the types of meaning that rank the highest in importance to you.

1. **Rewards and challenges:** something offered in exchange for service, to provide stimulation, renewal, or motivation (for example, money, awards, appreciation, applause, etc.). □

2. **Interesting field or industry:** working in an area of business that holds your attention or is somehow attractive, intriguing, or stimulating (for example, moving into investment banking from commercial banking). □

3. **Expressing ideals and values:** living by or communicating standards, principles, or qualities (for example, working for a company that openly supports women and minorities). □

4. **Contributing/making a difference:** to give, share, or participate, to change or improve (for example, implementing a program that motivates and gives incentives to employees). □

5. **Solving problems:** answering questions or handling situations that present difficulty, uncertainty, or complexity (for example, working as a mediator). □

6. **Changing your lifestyle:** alter or modify your values, priorities, relationships, etc. (for example, work from your home office in order to spend more time with your children). □

7. **Feeling passionate:** experience powerful emotion or appetite (for example, work for a cause that you strongly believe in). □

8. **Supporting a cause:** contribute time, resources, or expertise; advocate for change on behalf of the cause; promote or

advance the mission of a social or political movement or a needy or underserved population (for example, shift from a profit-making organization to nonprofit). ☐

9. **Innovating/creating:** introduce, produce, or imagine something new or original that contributes in some way to the general good (for example, start a company that sells environmentally sound items for the home). ☐

10. **Learning:** to gain knowledge, understanding, or expertise through experience or study (for example, lead a new project in an area that you or your company hasn't been involved with previously). ☐

These ten categories will provide you with a broad foundation from which you can better identify and describe the types of meaning that are most important to you. Look back at your answers to the questions on pages 63 and 64. Which of these fit into the ten categories you just read? If, for example, one of your answers to question 1 on page 63 is "I started a new chapter of a professional association and increased the membership to 125 active members," a few of the categories of meaning that are important to you are contributing/making a difference, supporting a cause, and innovating/creating.

Analyze all of your answers this way to see if the same types of meaning keep cropping up as the most significant to you. Did your answers to the questions on pages 63 and 64 align with the types of meaning you checked in the second exercise on page 65 and this page as being important to you? As you move ahead in your quest for meaning in your work, refer back to the ten types of meaning and their descriptions, using them as a framework.

————

Judi, who is middle-aged, has had four careers. For the past twenty years she has been in sales. She has volunteered for various causes throughout her life and is often described by people who know her as a giving individual who cares about helping others. Judi loves sales, and she is very good at it. She has successfully sold telephones, real estate, marketing promotions, mortgages, and plush toys.

Despite her adjunct volunteer work and fondness for sales, Judi felt that she wanted to combine her avocation with her vocation and took a job selling assisted-living services. She felt that she finally had found her niche. She was elated at being able to combine sales with something that held meaning for her. Then an opportunity to enter the field of fund-raising for a high-quality health system surfaced and she decided to explore. Judi said that fund-raising combined "my love of sales with a desire to touch people's hearts. It is an incredible feeling to be able to walk through a hospital, cancer center, rehab center, hospice residence, or nursing home and know that your efforts are supporting the services being provided to patients both in compensated and uncompensated care." Although no longer in fund-raising she has remained in this health-care system and is now promoting their new health and fitness center. She said that she wished that she had realized earlier how putting the meaning in her work was what she needed for professional fulfillment and that happiness in your career is not derived from the money one earns or simply successfully meeting targeted sales goals.

Step 2: Explore Roadblocks and Opportunities

Now you will identify any obstacles or barriers, either real or perceived, that could become actual roadblocks to finding your meaning. Some examples are: There isn't enough learning potential; I'm too old; I don't have a degree; etc.

List them here:

_____

_____

Most of the barriers or obstacles you have written down may not actually be real but perceived. Below are some of the most common barriers people think would prevent them from changing their career to find more meaning.

"I'll have to take a decrease in pay."

This is the time to address the number-one fear people have about changing their career and/or industry—money! It is generally believed that if your brand of meaning involves working in the nonprofit world, or you want to switch to a new industry, you will have to take a significant decrease in pay. While it is common knowledge that the nonprofit world doesn't offer robust compensation packages, there is a valuable trade-off if making a difference or supporting a cause is important to you.

Bruce is an excellent example. For twenty-five years, he worked for a major New York City–based bank. Of those twenty-five years, he admits that he felt gratified for only eight, when he moved out of the audit and banking side of the business into an organizational development and training function. Yet, even during those eight good years, Bruce was never comfortable in banking, constantly feeling that "I wasn't getting what I wanted—it wasn't ever right." When he was given the opportunity to take a separation package because the bank was merging with another bank, fearful as he was, he took it. He went through outplacement and during that time did, as he called it, "a lot of housecleaning." He took a hard look at his personal values and realized that a sense of mission and making a difference was something he craved—and that it had been missing for much of his career. One day, Bruce attended a luncheon and listened to a panel of people who had successfully made the switch from the profit to the nonprofit world. Immediately, Bruce felt right at home. The proverbial "lightbulb" went on, and he knew that joining a nonprofit was clearly the path he needed to take.

After consulting for very little money or on a pro bono basis with various nonprofit organizations, Bruce was offered a job as chief financial officer of a New York City domestic violence agency. A victim of domestic violence himself while growing up, Bruce has never felt better or more fulfilled in his work. He's still number-crunching, but is also involved with strategy, and wears innumerable other hats at the agency. He is earning less money than he did at the bank and admits that his ego was a little fragile about this at first. Nevertheless, he would never change his situation for a larger salary. If Bruce wants to, he can do consulting work on the side, write articles, and do many other things to generate extra income. Overall, his work life is less stressful, which gives him extra time and energy to pursue more of his outside interests.

As for the perception that you will have to accept less money if you switch careers, this really depends upon how well you package yourself and your skills when you are "selling" yourself to potential employers or clients. Nici made a switch from being a marketing executive for an agency that worked with consumer products companies to a sales management position in the design field. Her current salary is comparable to her old one because she cleverly and effectively presented her management and marketing experience to her new employer. That and her obvious love of fashion and passionate interest in design easily convinced her new employer that Nici would be a great asset to the business.

"I'm too old."

While it is easy to look at certain fields or industries and fantasize about what it would be like to work in them—becoming a musician, an airline pilot, a sommelier, or an advertising executive—many of us stop ourselves from turning fantasy into reality by thinking of age as an obstacle. There are hundreds of stories about courageous individuals who dreamed of pursuing a career they had previously fantasized about and did it, despite being older. Even though the reality is that we live in a society that is biased against older people, the truth is that if you have the passion, drive, and courage to change your career at an advanced age, you can do it!

At the age of forty, with four children and limited previous work experience, Bernice went to law school. Her husband wasn't too thrilled about the idea at first, but Bernice was determined. While forty may not seem old to start a new career, most of Bernice's fellow law students were half her age. When she graduated from law school, Bernice worked for a law firm to gain experience and then started her own firm. Today, she runs a successful law practice and has never been happier or more fulfilled. She gets deep satisfaction from making a difference in her clients' lives by fighting for their rights, whether in a real estate deal or a divorce. She thinks she's a better attorney now than she would have been had she gone to law school before or during the time she was raising a family, simply because she's wiser and more mature now.

If you've written down "I'm too old" or "The corporate world discriminates against people my age," think again. These may be accurate statements if your dream is to become a pitcher for the New York Yankees or the hottest new model in Paris. There are always going to be companies and people in the world who favor youth in the workplace. But if you have the drive and have done your homework to learn about the industry that you are passionate about, nothing should prevent you from becoming a part of it.

"I don't have specific industry experience."

You may believe that having little or no experience is something that can hold you back from going into a new industry. While you may not be familiar with the business you are interested in, you do have plenty of experience and skills from doing many other things. Business is business regardless of which industry you're in. There are always clients, customers, and stakeholders. Every business has sales, marketing, finance, human resources, product/service development, and operational needs. Goals and the need to achieve results are also standard issues in the business world.

Remember the ex-banker, Bruce? While he was very interested in moving from profit to nonprofit, he didn't want to take the time to learn how to manage a nonprofit or become a fundraiser, as sales didn't interest him. Instead, he applied his accounting and finance skills to the nonprofit world. Yes, there was a slight learning curve for him, but it wasn't as dramatic as he originally had thought it might be. He was patient about finding the right nonprofit opportunity, first learning about the business while consulting and offering his services as a volunteer. When he stepped on board as CFO, he was ahead of the game from a knowledge standpoint. His employer appreciates the different perspective that Bruce brings to their operation and feels fortunate to have an ex-banker on his staff.

Learning about a new industry can be exciting and challenging, particularly if it's one that you've always thought about or leaned toward. Volunteering for a business, doing part-time consulting, or sitting on a board or advisory council are wonderfully effective ways to get an education. Every industry has trade publications and industry-specific associations that hold regular meetings and publish newsletters. The Resources guide at the end of this book can help you to identify some of them. Informational interviews are an excellent method for learning about a new industry. Networking with people to get the names of professionals who work in a specific industry, and compiling the same list of questions for each person, is a great information-gathering technique. Ask questions like: "How did you get into this field?" "What credentials, skills, and experience do you believe would be helpful for someone wishing to enter this field?" "I've described my background and some of my major accomplishments to you. Which do you think are particularly transferable to your industry?" "What are the most significant problems that you and people in your field are facing today?"

When people see that you are passionate and have spent time trying to learn about their industry, they will be much more inclined to reveal opportunities and introduce you to decision-makers.

"I don't know how to find a company that will allow me to express my ideals and values."

One of the obstacles you face may be your lack of knowledge about the type of industry, company, or environment that would support your values and ideals. Because you've taken the values self-assessment, you already know whether or not those values are being supported in your current work. If you hold tight to what is important to you, you will become more skilled at finding a work situation that will meet your needs in this area.

Ed is a perfect example. A human resource professional in his late forties, Ed had worked for a series of companies that failed to support diversity. As a gay man, Ed constantly felt discomfort at having to work in an environment where he couldn't openly acknowledge his sexual preference. He also knew that his employer, a major investment house, was uncomfortable with the gay and lesbian community. Ed's key value is to have the freedom to express his sexual preference openly. For the first time in his life, he approached his job search with this important personal value uppermost in his mind.

Ed ended up at a smaller firm in the PR business that openly supports gays in the workplace. How did he do it? He networked through a gay friend who is head of human resources at this firm. His friend persuaded the leadership to bring Ed on board in a higher-level human resources role than they originally thought they needed. By taking the time to find out what really matters to him, and believing that it could happen, Ed landed a job that resonates with who he is as a person. Like Judi and Bruce and Bernice, he has never been happier or more fulfilled by work.

When exploring companies or industries with an eye toward whether or not you'll be able to fulfill your values, you must ask tough questions—and be prepared to accept the answers. In Ed's situation, many firms professed to support diversity, but they really didn't, at least not to Ed's satisfaction. The better the job you do at investigating a company to find out whether or not its values—and practices—are really in sync with your own, the more likely you will be to discover the truth. When trying to explore these types of concerns, ask questions such as:

How would you describe the corporate culture here?

Recognition is a value that is important to me; can you give me examples of how the company gives recognition to its employees?

If a company resists having you talk to others besides their designated interviewing team, beware.

Sean worked for ten years as a very successful attorney with a large insurance conglomerate. While there, he was involved in a complex litigation matter, a massive refinancing, a sale of a significant business, and the purchase of an HMO. These projects sustained Sean well from the standpoint of professional challenge and the ability to contribute, solve problems, and creatively collaborate with colleagues and clients. Unfortunately, his employer's values began to change noticeably, and Sean felt as if the company he worked for was no longer in alignment with his own values and belief systems. His core belief in the importance of integrity, honesty, and family values had always motivated Sean to become involved in significant pro bono work, an activity that his company had always encouraged and even made possible for him to do, but now such opportunities were becoming scarcer. Although he was presented with many additional opportunities within the organization when he expressed his discontent to senior management, he chose to leave and join a real estate development company whose values supported his own, as vice president of community relations.

"I can't make a difference."

Most human beings want to feel that they are either contributing to a greater cause or are having a positive impact on people or a process. One of the most common concerns people have is that, although they would like to become involved in something where they will find this kind of meaning, they don't feel they can have a significant impact, either financially or from an energy or time standpoint. Experiencing boredom in your job and feeling as if there is no meaning to your work are often connected. On July 2, 2000, the *New York Times* ran an article with the headline WANTED: BORED PROFESSIONALS WHO HAVE TEACHING IN MIND. The article described a campaign that New York City had launched to recruit 250 professionals with no teaching experience to teach in the city's most troubled schools. Among the four hundred people who applied were bankers, lawyers, a judge, a speechwriter, and business people who, as the schools chancellor Harold O. Levy said, "are people who have decided the job they are doing is not spiritually satisfying."

If you are working in a job in which you don't feel as if you are really contributing or making a difference, take a look around you. What needs to be changed, improved, revitalized, or eliminated? Nothing is perfect, and there is always room for improvement or development. Make it your mission to undertake this kind of project. If the people you work with don't want this kind of help from you, then it may be time to look for a new work situation where you *can* make a difference. As Sean, the attorney who left the insurance industry, says of his new career in real estate, "I have the opportunity to combine and apply so many of my skills in the context of projects that make a real and substantial difference to communities."

You have special qualities, strengths, and skills that you enjoy using. Instead of thinking about what the world needs, reverse your thinking and identify the ways in which you can help a coworker, a group, a cause, or an organization by using your unique talents.

Janet is fifty-three and has had eight careers. She has been a teacher, an arbitrator, and a conservation technician in a museum, and she owned her own events company—to name a few. Currently, she works as the director of volunteers for a nonprofit agency for children. While doing volunteer work at the agency, she took a look around, thought about her skills and what she likes to do, and drew up a job description. She then approached the agency and convinced them that this role was needed and that she was the best candidate for it. Janet loves her job. "I work part-time," she explains. "I am continuing to build upon experiences and skills I brought to this position and am learning new skills at the same time. Perfect!"

"I'm not sure how I'll solve problems in an industry I've never worked in before."

Sometimes you may not be sure that you are capable of solving a problem in an area in which you have no expertise or within an industry you don't know. The plus side of trying to solve problems in a field that is new to you is that you don't possess the habits and routine behavior patterns that often obscure the vision of someone who has worked closely in a particular industry. You can add a fresh perspective.

Gail had a long career in sales management for several large companies, and though she enjoyed it, she realized that she was tired of the day-to-day tedium of managing people. She decided to strike out on her own as a consultant working with privately held businesses. Gail always got excited about solving problems and when she started helping small businesses solve their sales problems, she really felt as if she had found her niche.

"I don't know if I can change my lifestyle."

If you're like most people who work, you probably feel as if you don't have enough time in the day to get everything done either at work or in your personal life. You may even tend to push your family to the end of your "to do" list in deference to your job and your boss. You may be exhausted, yet you just aren't sure how you can change the way you are living.

Howard was laid off in the mid-1990s from an executive job on Wall Street. After a month of not working, he commented to his outplacement counselor how impressed he was with his wife and children. He never knew who they were "as people" during his years of working on Wall Street, and couldn't ever imagine letting his relationships with his family erode again. Although fearful that he wouldn't be able to earn the same amount of money, he researched franchises and bought one that sells juice to small companies. After a year and a half, he was back to his old Wall Street salary. Sure, he had to work hard to build his business, but the flexibility he now has to spend time with his family has made a world of difference.

"I don't really feel passionate about anything."

If you've never truly felt passion for anything in your work, your greatest obstacle may well be finding out what it is that will give you this feeling. While it isn't necessary to be passionate, and most people aren't all the time, those who have taken the time to uncover their passion are truly happy, excited, and satisfied, and view work in the same light as play. In *The Passion Plan,* Richard Chang outlines a seven-step model for bringing passion into your life. He describes passion as either content- or context-based. Examples of content-based passion are activities like golf, fishing, computers, or cooking, while context-based passions are centered on themes like improvement, leading, entrepreneurship, or competition. We can experience both types of passion in our work and in other areas.

While there may be something that you feel passionate about, if it's a hobby or extracurricular activity, you probably think that it can't be woven into your work life. If you are a golfer, it is unrealistic to think that you can give up your day job and join the PGA tour! Yet, you may be able to bring your passion for golf into your work. Frank, for example, works for a real estate management company, managing buildings all over the United States, and plays golf with half a dozen of the building managers. He has been able to combine earning a nice living with playing golf with his clients as often as he likes.

Think about what you feel passionate about. Is it something you are involved with outside of work? Is it something that you haven't been involved with in a long time? Is it something that you do at work, but not enough to keep those passionate feelings ignited? Sit down with a piece of paper and write down all the ways that you can incorporate your passion into your work. For the moment, forget any limitations that you may perceive. Or gather a small group of friends together and have a brainstorming session to generate ideas about how you can integrate passion into your work.

Not sure what your passion is? Start looking at the world through different eyes. What interests you that you've never done before? Is there an activity or hobby that you've always been drawn to but never tried? Why not find someone who does it and ask him or her to show you the ropes? Take a class or a workshop to see if it really turns you on. Whether you are interested in archery or running your own business, the only way to discover your passion is to try it!

Don waited until he retired to pursue his passion, which is teaching math to high school kids at a private school. He worked in corporate America for years, then sold insurance before "retiring" to teach math. "Yes! I am satisfied with my work," he says.

"I wake up each morning looking forward to going to school. The students are challenging and fun to be with, and I love my subject."

"I don't have enough time."

In a survey of doctors, lawyers, engineers, and other high-profile executives conducted by *umbershoot.net,* 94 percent of those surveyed said that their dream was to help mankind. While many of us fantasize about doing good and helping the less fortunate, many of us think there's not enough time to do so. Another survey conducted by a nonprofit consortium showed that 52 percent of the United States population volunteers in community service for an average of five hours a week. If you increasingly feel the need to add meaning to your life by supporting a cause but feel that you just don't have enough time to give, here are some suggestions.

To match your interests and skills with an organization in need of what you can offer, try looking at these Web sites: *volunteermatch.org* and *helping.org.* The Resources guide at the back of this book also lists nonprofit and charity organizations that you can contact. If you are interested in supporting a cause and earning a living doing it, consider volunteer work first so that you can get a feeling for the way nonprofit organizations operate.

Of course, finding the time to volunteer is a real problem for people who work full-time. If you are someone who needs a more structured schedule, then commit to doing something at the same time every other week. If you prefer spontaneity, then volunteer for an organization that doesn't need for you to be there consistently at the same place and same time but is more interested in whatever effort or creative contribution you can provide. Start small, offering your time and talents in limited doses. If you work for an employer who supports programs in the community, get involved through this avenue first. Or approach your company and ask them to sponsor you in a volunteer effort by giving you flexible hours or time off.

Bill was an engineer for fifteen years and, although he liked tinkering and was good at testing, he really didn't enjoy his work. He left engineering and moved into information services and general management in the telecommunications field. After five years, he was laid off and took the summer to reflect upon what he wanted to do. He and his wife, Mary, had volunteered part-time for many years and Mary's career was already in the nonprofit sector. After a serious discussion with his wife, Bill decided to volunteer for a number of community organizations. Today, he works as a volunteer ambulance attendant, a volunteer fireman, and as a volunteer for a food collection organization. He sits on the board of an agency that donates clothing and food to low-income families, works for a food bank, and is the chairperson of his church's Christmas tree sale. In addition, he loves to sing and is a member of a choral society and a male a cappella group. He generates income from three of these activities and says, "I'm fifty-six and it seems that a lot of people I know are doing things that aren't making them happy. We, on the other hand, are having a lot of fun!"

"I'm not very creative."

As adults, we can sometimes be apprehensive or feel insecure about our ability to be creative. We convince ourselves that creativity is only for children. But with technology taking over so many of our left-brain tasks, we have more of an opportunity to create and innovate. Unfortunately, we can get so mired in day-to-day tasks and deadlines that we don't make creativity a priority. We tell ourselves it's something that we will do when we "retire" or when we go on vacation.

Creativity takes so many forms—it's not just sculpting, painting, or writing. Julia Cameron wrote a wonderful book called *The Artist's Way*, in which she presents a step-by-step method for discovering and recovering your creative self. Cameron talks about taking your creative potential seriously by stopping negative talk such as: "It's too late," "My friends and family will think I'm crazy," or "Creativity is a luxury and I should be grateful for what I've got." Although she wrote the book for aspiring and working artists, it is one that anyone can read to unleash the creative spirit lying dormant in all of us.

Creativity means being innovative, original, or imaginative. In the context of your current job, is there a way that you can focus more on these kinds of activities and less on the routine "business as usual" tasks? Do you have one idea that you've been thinking about for years but that you've never had the courage or taken the time to pursue?

Angie is a midlevel human resources professional at a nonprofit organization. While she fulfills her need for meaning, making a contribution, expressing her values, and supporting a cause very successfully in her job, she is constantly thinking of and inventing new products unrelated to her work. She has explored getting patents and manufacturing several of her innovations but always stops short of following through because of time, money, or family obligations. The next step for Angie should be to identify one invention, and put a plan together to get a patent, find financing for manufacturing a demo of the product, and create a marketing plan. She can approach the Service Corps of Retired Executives (a nonprofit organization of retired executives who provide coaching to entrepreneurs, *www.score.com*) to help her with the process so she doesn't have to pay someone to give her advice. Until Angie does these things, she will feel frustrated and unfulfilled despite the satisfaction she derives from her job.

Becoming the next Mozart, Rembrandt, or Shakespeare isn't what drives most people who seek to express themselves creatively, although feeling that you don't have the kind of talent those famous artists possessed may be impeding you. If you need to be more creative and innovative, the form or venue is irrelevant. What is relevant is the fact that you yearn to be more creative and you should not wait until you have "the time or money" to do so.

Step 3: Create an Action Plan

Now it's time to fill out a simple action plan to help you in your search to find meaning in your work. Here is Angie's to use as an example:

The kind of meaning I want to pursue is:
Innovating/creating: I'd like to sell my thermal lunch bag in catalogs and discount stores.

**The short-term action steps (tasks/activities)
I will take are:**

1. Contact the office of patents to learn about the process for securing a patent for my lunch bag.

   When will I get this done? By November 15.

2. Contact the Service Corps of Retired Executives (SCORE) to find a counselor who can help me with my business plan for launching my lunch bag.

   When will I get this done? By November 30.

3. Go through the steps of applying for a patent for my lunch bag, filling out all the necessary paperwork and sending it in.

   When will I get this done? By January 31.

4. With the help of my SCORE adviser, write a business plan.

   When will I get this done? By February 28.

Now fill out your action plan. Although it may change based upon the research you do or information you need, by putting your short-term goals on paper, you will feel more committed to doing what you have to in order to create the meaning you are yearning for in your work.

ACTION PLAN

The meaning I want to pursue is:

_____

_____

_____

_____

_____

The short-term action steps (tasks/activities) I will take are:

1. _____

_____

_____

_____

When will I get this done?_____

2. _____

_____

_____

_____

When will I get this done?_____

3. _____

_____

_____

_____

When will I get this done?_____

4. _____

_____

_____

When will I get this done?_____

    Meaning is different for each of us. Without meaning in your work, whether it's one of the ten categories in this chapter, or something that you've identified that isn't on the list, the only thing keeping you from finding it and making it happen is you. Whether it's a question of time, money, talent, attitude, drive, technical ability, knowledge, or interest—or your perception that any or all of these things can't or don't exist—there are plenty of resources to help you overcome your obstacles. Think about the kinds of meaning that are missing for you right now and start small by exploring how to add meaning to your work. Identify one thing that you can do to add meaning to your work, whether it's doing something creative, volunteering your time, researching an industry that you find interesting, or solving a problem that has been plaguing you at work. The joy and satisfaction awaiting you are indescribable.

Been There, Done That, but Still Need to Earn

Tom is a vice president of human resources for a health-care contract research firm. At fifty-three, he has made seven job changes since graduating from college, all within the human resources field. While he enjoys a large degree of independence, professional challenge, and satisfaction, he says, "I'd like the challenge of a new career. The reality is, however, that I am at a level both professionally and financially that is difficult to give up. That, and the age of my children, will likely keep me from pursuing an alternative career for another ten years."

If you are like Tom, this chapter is for you. You're enjoying a successful career but can't imagine continuing to do the kind of work that you've been doing for a long time. But, and there is a big "but" here, you really need to continue earning the same amount of money or more, for a given period of time or even indefinitely.

Many people in the workforce feel the way Tom does. If you are one of them, take a leap of faith and buy into the philosophy that hope and possibilities exist *if* you uncover your true interests and are willing to begin to plan the next phase of your work. Yes, there is a next phase, but only if you believe there is and are

willing to do whatever it takes to make it happen. If not, you will continue to sit in your job feeling stale and trapped.

Step 1: Complete the "Been There, Done That, but Still Need to Earn" Self-Assessment

First, make an action plan folder labeled "The Work I'm Going to Do Next" and keep it somewhere within reach—not stashed away in a drawer in your desk! You'll need it to be easily accessible so that you can refer to it later.

Go back and look at the results of all the self-assessments you took in chapters 3 and 4. Begin by reviewing the values self-assessment on page 31.

Now do the same with the attitudes self-assessment on pages 33–37. Are there one or two areas that you can work on within this self-assessment? Review the six categories within the attitude self-assessment. On the lines provided below, write down what you think you can do to improve your attitude in each category, keeping in mind the values that are important to you. I've made some suggestions to help you get started. Being proactive about shifting your attitude will help you to jumpstart the process of moving out of your Been There, Done That, but Still Need to Earn situation.

Self-confidence
In what ways can you improve your self-confidence?

Suggestion: Focus on one skill, such as networking, and practice it. Identify three new people you can meet, call them and schedule a face-to-face meeting.

_____

_____

_____

_____

Self-knowledge

How can you improve your self-knowledge?

Suggestion: Ask three people who know you in different ways for feedback about something specific, such as the way you present yourself.

_____

_____

_____

_____

Managing Relationships

In what ways can you better manage your relationships?

Suggestion: Talk to a client, a friend, and your child or spouse about your relationships and what they'd like to get from them that may not exist now.

_____

_____

_____

_____

Maintaining Motivation

How can you better maintain your motivation?

Suggestion: Set a reasonable goal for yourself for something that you need to change or improve, such as time management or organization. Put a simple plan together with a time line for completing your plan. Document your progress.

_____

_____

_____

_____

Goal Orientation

How can you make yourself more goal-oriented?

Suggestion: Set one simple goal, such as finishing this book or writing in a journal every day for a week.

_____

_____

_____

_____

Professional Commitment

In what ways can you deepen your professional commitment?

Suggestion: Read two trade publications (which are probably sitting in your office somewhere) in the next five days. Share one piece of information with someone else in your company or field.

_____

_____

_____

_____

Now review your results for the rest of the self-assessments you took, including your personality preferences, your score on the change readiness quiz, what your primary interests are, and your favorite skills.

Write down any and all titles, jobs, types of work, names of companies and industries where you think you could possibly fulfill your values, top interests, personality preferences, and favorite skills. Use brainstorming techniques to do this: Write down as many ideas as come to your mind, whether they seem realistic or not. Try not to allow biases, prejudices, perceptions, or even concrete obstacles to negatively color your brainstorming process. Keep writing down words and phrases until you've run out of ideas. List them one by one on each line.

For example, Leslie wrote, "Disney, MTV, Christie's [auction house], Amazon.com, museums, interior decorator, my own business, author, architect, nonprofit, teach kids art, botanical gardens, travel writer, chef."

_____

_____

_____

_____

_____

_____

_____

_____

_____

_____

Now you are going to prioritize your thoughts and ideas based on *your level of interest*.

1. Starting with the number 1, rank every single word or phrase that you've written down by writing a large number next to it on the left side. Once again, don't think about your

prejudices, lack of knowledge, or negative perceptions while you are prioritizing. Go with your gut. Don't spend too much time thinking about this exercise—just do it.

2. Do the same thing again, only this time write the number on the right side. Rank your words and phrases based upon *how realistic it is that you can make this idea happen* (with the number 1 representing the most realistic).

In the second exercise, do not think about realism in the context of the present. Frame it in terms of "someday." By doing this, you will avoid assessing the "realism" factor in terms of your ability to meet your current personal expenses. On the other hand, the amount of money you may have to spend to make your goal happen *is* part of the realism factor. Let's say, for example, you wrote down, "Buy a seat on the New York Stock Exchange." In February 2001, a seat on the New York Exchange sold for $2 million and there are a total of only 1,366 seats, mostly unavailable. Therefore, while your interest level may be high, your realism ranking is not, because of the high cost of entry and the limited availability of seats.

When you finish these exercises, review your lists carefully and look for any surprises or common themes. What are they? Do the job titles, industries, and work you prioritized as your top-five interests match any of the five that led the list when you prioritized them from a reality perspective?

Now, look at your list of top values, interests, and motivated abilities from the assessment you took and compare it to your top-five job, industry, or work interests. Based on the knowledge you have, will these things provide you with what you want and need? We'll come back to this later on in this chapter.

Step 2: Explore Roadblocks and Opportunities

Having a career plan in place—with practical, achievable goals—significantly increases the probability of realizing these goals. Otherwise, you might sit and stagnate for another two or three years.

Let's explore the financial aspects of your situation. As popular financial-planning guru Suze Orman says in her best-selling book *The Nine Steps to Financial Freedom,* "It is never too soon to begin, and it is never too late to start." If you are dealing with exorbitant expenses, undoubtedly this is creating stress for you and your family. Revisiting your finances to learn where you can make sensible changes can only help to relieve this stress.

Start by making an appointment with a financial planner. Be sure to find one through a personal referral from someone whose judgment you trust. Also be sure to choose someone who is truly skilled at putting a plan together for you and is not just interested in selling stocks or mutual funds. Be prepared to fill out a "Net Cash Flow Form" that shows your monthly expenses and income. A good financial planner will also help you understand your net worth and comprehend your tax situation more clearly. While you may have met with a financial planner before or have investments for which you receive advice, it is unlikely that you have ever *tied financial planning into your career* before. Most people tend to keep these two very important aspects of their lives separate until something happens, such as the sudden loss of a job. You need to know which of your assets and financial investments you may have to use in order to finance a new venture, such as starting a business or changing careers.

If the top-five jobs or industries you elicited from your brainstorming session are not at all related to your current job, then you probably aren't assured of being able to earn at your current level. In fact, most people automatically assume that if they switch fields or start a business, they will have to accept a drastic cut in pay. This doesn't always turn out to be true. Whether it's true or not, and you know you will disappoint yourself if you don't make a career change at some point, it's time for you to become familiar with your expenses, cash flow, and entire financial picture so that you can plan accordingly.

Some expenses, such as college tuition or alimony payments, are fixed for a definite period of time. Others, such as special education and treatment for a disability or an elderly parent in an assisted-living residence, are more difficult to plug into a time frame. Regardless of which categories your expenses fall into, you should tell your financial planner that you are planning to change careers. He or she will help you to set financial goals aligned with your needs so that you can make a financially sound change.

Remember Tom, the human resources executive who believed that being financially responsible for his children would prevent him from pursuing a new career for another ten years? In ten years, Tom will be sixty-three, and while many people are still vibrant and interested in learning new things at that age, both Tom's energy and career interests will be dramatically different by then.

If you are like Tom, what should you do? In addition to completing the assessment at the opening of the chapter and consulting with a financial planner, you should also examine the less tangible aspects of money. What are your attitudes about it? How important is earning a good salary to you, beyond your financial responsibility to your family? Author Suze Orman hones in on these "softer" aspects of dealing with money, helping readers become aware of how they were raised to think about dealing with money and what's at the root of their specific financial habits, like spending and saving.

Review the options available to you for reconfiguring your present job if you haven't already. Go through the exercise of writing down every one of the jobs you have held since college and identify three things:

1. Your level of satisfaction in the role and the reasons for it (whether you were satisfied or not).
2. Your greatest one or two accomplishments while in each position.

3. The strengths and skills you learned/used to achieve these accomplishments.

Once you have identified these things, you will see some consistent themes for what makes you feel happy and satisfied in your work, and what does not. Write down these themes and then look at your current position and think about ways you can increase the factors that bring you job satisfaction or how to find them without changing jobs.

You should also do what many people do—look at ways to fulfill your interests outside your job. Eventually, an outside interest or activity can turn into a full-time job—with pay!

Sue is a good example of this. For seven years, she has worked as a public relations coordinator for a nonprofit organization. When she had been in her full-time position for about three years, she started her own public relations business on the side and has accumulated fifty or so clients with whom she works at different times. Sue is a widow and wants to feel more financially comfortable before launching her own business on a full-time basis, which is her goal. While Sue does not quite fall into the Been There, Done That category, she is a good example of someone who has cautiously planned her next career because of her need to earn enough money. She also falls into the Yearning to Be on Your Own category, and by building her business on a part-time basis while earning a regular paycheck, she is satisfying this need as well.

Most people can use the counsel of an outside expert to help them make tough but meaningful changes in their lives. At forty-three, Alison has worked in the publishing industry her entire career. Not only does she feel worn out from working in the same field for so long, but also she admits that she never has been happy in publishing.

"Though I like business, I'm not really the corporate type," Alison says. "I like to learn about what makes people tick. I don't care about fifteen-million-dollar annual quotas. I focus too much stress and energy on a large entity that does not acknowledge me as a person or recognize my talents as an individual . . . such as my communication skills, sense of humor, and holistic approach to doing business.

"I want to start my own thing," she explains "but am so multifaceted that I don't know how to create one thing, and I don't have the cash to create it. But I'm not giving up!"

What Alison needs to do is focus on some viable career options and develop a financial plan, which will help her overcome the obstacle of not having enough money.

Step 3: Create an Action Plan

Now it's time for you to create a plan with concrete steps that will move you out of your Been There, Done That mode.

Your plan should answer the following questions:

• What are all of the career or work paths that interest you and are realistic? While the realism factor may not be obvious if you haven't yet investigated what is required to enter a specific field, you'll still be able to make some guesses about this. You can narrow your list down later once you've gathered more information. For now, you may want to focus on the list of jobs and industries you prioritized earlier in this chapter.

• What kind of research do you need to do to learn more about what is entailed in the work you've deemed interesting? To find the answers to this question, you might network at trade association meetings, set up informational meetings with people who work in the job or industry that you're interested in, go on interviews, search the Internet, or visit the reference section of the library. While researching the quantifiable aspects of work, such as salaries and educational requirements, is important, the best information comes from talking to people who do the kind of work you think you want to do. Create a list of questions that you can ask everyone you meet so that you will be prepared and will remember everything you heard. Having a list will also help you to compare the answers you hear to form your own conclusions. Questions you can ask:

How did you get into this field?

What experience or characteristics do you think I'm lacking?

What are my advantages?

What suggestions do you have for identifying job opportunities?

• What is a pragmatic time line for moving into another career? Much of your decision about this will depend upon the plan that you and your financial planner create. Without a plan, you won't be able to be specific about your time frame for achieving your career goals. Make sure to factor in the time it will take to prepare for and launch your new career. Depending on your situation, this will include things like getting a degree or certification, finding real estate space, conducting a job search, and the legal processes involved with transactions like buying a franchise or a business. Any of these can take six months to a year to accomplish. If you've really decided that you absolutely cannot change careers for, say, another four years (perhaps you're not really being realistic), you should still put an action plan in place to help you deal with your Been There, Done That symptoms. Your plan may include learning new skills, working toward a new role within your company or industry, or improving your competence in an outside hobby.

Here are some additional steps to creating an effective action plan:

• Create criteria for yourself that will help you to decide when and why you might stop exploring a specific career path. Angela sold shoes from the time she graduated from college. When she was thirty-eight, she started to question how fulfilled she was at her job and "wondered if I could continue to sell shoes to retail stores between Washington and Boston for the next twenty-two years. But what else could I do? My family depends on me to provide forty percent of the income needed to keep our lifestyle going. I explored becoming a teacher, but the study period was too long and there wasn't enough money in it. I also explored opening my own business as a Kindermusik or Music Together franchisee, but there was already a lot of competition for children's activities in my geographic area and they could not give me a franchise in the areas I wanted. I looked into opening my own not-for-profit corporation to help educate and empower the needy but decided I would be too much at the mercy of private and public foundations." Although the results were disappointing for Angela, because she had spent time assessing her own needs and desires carefully, it was easier for her to walk away from a possible career option as soon as it became clear that it would not meet her criteria.

• Create a realistic time line for each of the goals in your plan. Since you aren't trying to make a career change tomorrow, don't try to do too much at once or you will feel overwhelmed and probably give up on your search. Perhaps doing one research activity every two weeks would make sense for you. On the other hand, since you don't have an immediate sense of urgency, it's very important to set goals to keep you on track, using your goals and deadlines as motivation to keep you going.

• Find someone to confide in and share what you are doing. Ask this person to be your informal coach and to check in with you periodically to find out how you're doing with your plan so that you'll feel accountable to someone other than yourself.

• Keep an open mind to possibilities that may not have occurred to you. Despite all of her exploration, Angela, the persistent shoe salesperson, didn't feel any closer to identifying a new career until a client of hers who owned a shoe store passed away suddenly at age forty-two. Her client had not planned for a premature death, and his shoe store was the only source of income for his family. His wife did not know how to run the business on her own, so their son quit college to run the store to support the family. Her late client's misfortune was an eye-opener for Angela. "I couldn't believe how a lack of planning could effectively disrupt an entire family's hopes and dreams for the future so thoroughly," she recalls. It was then that Angela realized she could use her desire to help and teach others by pursuing an occupation that could be both personally and financially rewarding. She became a financial representative for an insurance and financial company—a career path that had never before occurred to her.

• Start scheduling networking and informational meetings to gather information and meet people. In chapter 12, you'll learn specific tips on how to network. Networking is one of the most useful business skills you can develop. Start your networking process with people with whom you feel most comfortable. If you don't know anyone in the jobs or fields that interest you, you'll have to find them first. Do this by making a list of ten or fifteen people whom you trust and who seem well connected to diverse groups of people. It doesn't matter what the people you network with do for a living, it matters whom they know. Everyone knows someone.

• When you are gathering information about a field or industry, don't just speak to one person who works in the area you've targeted. Every time you meet with someone, ask him or her for two names of people in their industry whom you might call or e-mail. Meet with half a dozen people who have varying levels of experience (not just senior-level people) so that you can see the complete picture. Ask questions like:

What do you enjoy about your job and your industry?

What do you dislike?

What are the three things you'd recommend I do to get into your field?

What are the dominant skills that you use most frequently in your job?

Who are the players in your industry that I should meet?

Nick was unemployed. Although he had worked in technical support in the telecommunications industry, he had always had a strong interest in real estate and even had some experience managing family property. He decided to investigate what he needed to do to become a property manager in commercial real estate. He started networking to find people in commercial real estate with whom he could talk. He set up his first informational meeting with a real estate broker. During their conversation, the broker made the offhand comment that property managers are all in their late twenties and early thirties. Nick, forty-nine, was gripped by a feeling of insecurity when he heard this and immediately stopped networking. Based on one offhand remark, Nick decided that he would never get a job as a real estate property manager because he was too old. If Nick had continued networking, he might have learned that this simply wasn't the reality; even if it were, he'd eventually meet or be referred to someone who liked Nick and would be in a position to help him pursue his dream. Although your networking should be targeted, you also need lots of people so you can hit the jackpot with the right job opportunity.

Keep a file or notebook exclusively for all of the information and names you gather, or create a contact list on your computer with your network's names and notes about your meetings with these new people.

While you are networking with people and gathering information about industries that interest you, be very inquisitive about the future trends that are taking place within those industries. The World Future Society *(www.wfs.org)* publishes a magazine about trends in the future called *The Futurist*, which covers work, business, and industry trends. If you are not planning on moving into your new career for several years, it is important to be aware of the ways that things could change, either positively or negatively.

Once you've gathered enough information to know whether or not it's realistic for you to plan on moving into a particular career, here are some things you can and should do to maintain your interest in your potential new career and accelerate your success once you actually do make your move:

• Is a specific degree or certification needed or strongly recommended for your new career? If there is, can you begin studying now on a part-time basis?

• Are there skills that you know you will need to strengthen or that you've never used that you can begin to work on now? If your plan is to open your own business, for example, and you don't have a clue about accounting or sales, why not take some classes at your local college or university?

• Can you arrange to work part-time at night or on weekends in the field you are interested in, either in a barter situation or for a nominal amount of money, so that you can learn?

• During your networking process, have you met someone who you think would be a good mentor or coach for you? Many people are flattered to be asked to be a mentor, especially if their investment of time won't be too significant. This is a great way to start learning about a new business.

You may not be able to eliminate or even diminish your financial obligations right now, but you are still in control of planning for your future and, most important, of ending your Been There, Done That blues.

CHAPTER 7

Bruised and Gun-shy

It will come as no great revelation to you that working is difficult. Whether you have always worked for large corporations or for a mix of small and medium-sized privately held companies, you probably have a horror story to tell about a specific job situation. Whether you have been laid off, discriminated against, or had to deal with a psychotic boss, you are affected adversely both while you're involved in the situation and after you leave, whether you realize it or not. Not only can your negative experience color your outlook about new work opportunities, but it can also prevent you from moving forward in your job search or career when you really need to.

In her book *Are You a Corporate Refugee?,* which she calls "a survival guide for downsized, disillusioned, and displaced workers," psychotherapist Ruth Luban tells dozens of stories about individuals who have been "innocent victims of business forces beyond their control." The book is packed with tips, resources, and suggestions for healing and moving through specific "recovery stages" to an eventual period of renewal and new beginnings.

While it is extremely important to deal with what has happened to you and put it into perspective, it is equally important to move on, to identify and engage in a type of work situation that is best for you. This chapter is for you if you're a "corporate refugee"—you need to recover and you need to work.

Melody is an insurance underwriter who retired early, presumably to keep her husband company because he had already retired. She admitted later that after taking two years off "to retire," the real reason she dropped out of the workforce is because she "felt beaten." "The worst thing for me was the eighteen months I spent in the job I had." Melody explains, "It truly was an environment where I felt personally attacked. I never should have stayed. I would not have stood for that abuse at age thirty or forty but I let it happen at forty-eight or fifty. I lost all my confidence at that job. So two years ago, at fifty-three, I restarted. If this new job doesn't turn out as promised, I won't stay this time. I expect to be treated as well as I treat people and I want the money."

It's not surprising to discover that people aren't very comfortable admitting that they feel Bruised and Gun-shy. Perhaps they feel it isn't professionally appropriate to admit that a negative experience has affected them adversely or that they might be viewed as "damaged goods." Whatever someone's reasons are for not admitting that they were defeated by their specific work experience, the fact remains that at one point or another, it happens to most of us. The important thing is to be able to deal with your emotions and feelings about what happened to you. Until you do this effectively, it will be tough to move on.

Suzanne, an administrator in the nonprofit sector, was terminated—unfairly, she thought—because she did not have a master's degree and the executive director said she needed one. She was upset, not only because she loved her job, but also because she felt she excelled at it. She also thought that age discrimination was at play in the executive director's decision to fire her. It took more than a year for Suzanne to recover. Her assessment of the workplace today? "It is complicated, to say the least! We have a workforce where mediocrity is the rule. Loyalty is practically nonexistent. Moreover, youth means everything, even though experience may be lacking. Workers over the age of forty-five are not desirable nor, in many cases, are they respected by coworkers and managers. Things are not changing on that front in spite of what's being said by the media. I and others I've met have personally experienced situations where concern about upsetting the chemistry of a team is of the greatest concern—not what you know or how you may help—especially when the team members are between twenty-five and thirty-four. I'm fifty-five—need I say more?"

While age discrimination was Suzanne's issue, feeling Bruised and Gun-shy can happen at any age or time in your career. Jillian was laid off from her first job out of college at a television station because her boss, the director of research, was forced into early retirement. So Jillian's position as her assistant also became extinct. She was then fired from her next job at a radio station because her computer skills weren't up to snuff. At the tender age of twenty-three, Jillian was Bruised and Gun-shy. Although her college degree was in broadcasting and it had never occurred to her that she would do anything else for a living, the thought of finding yet another job in a field where Jillian felt as if she was "not a very good fit" was not appealing. Her next job after the radio station was as a contingency recruiter for an employment agency. It was the beginning of a long and happy career in sales for Jillian.

Resources and support are important—and available—to help you deal with your emotional state about your painful work situation. Seeing a counselor or therapist can help you understand and sort out your emotions much more quickly than trying to do it on your own.

Suzanne, now happily employed as a copy editor for a small publishing company where she is using many of the skills she used in nonprofit, also has some sage advice, which she has successfully followed herself: "Don't be too hard on yourself. Give yourself time to heal and don't carry the experience around with you. Move on! Spend some time being good to yourself. Getting terminated from a job happens to others every day, and it has not been known to kill anyone yet." She adds, "Remember, it's not always about you! Sometimes it's about your manager or something completely nonsensical that has nothing to do with the quality of your work or reality! And if you feel as if you have been illegally dismissed or discriminated against, contact the Department of Labor for advice." The Department of Labor has a division that deals with these issues specifically, and will answer your questions and determine whether intervention is an appropriate next step. They will also write letters on your behalf.

Ruth Luban has some additional recommendations for those who are Bruised and Gun-shy and having difficulty moving beyond this stage. She stresses the importance of working through the five stages she describes in her book:

1. **On the Brink:** When you know something is wrong and that you may soon be a "refugee."
2. **Letting Go:** When you leave your work situation and begin to grieve.
3. **In the Wilderness:** When you are "living in ambiguity and allowing for this period of time of not knowing."
4. **Seeing the Beacon:** You have ideas, experiment with things, and start to "see the light."
5. **In the New Land:** You have found firm footing and are beginning a new cycle of renewal in a new work situation.

Understanding and moving through these five cycles will help you to normalize the emotional experience of being Bruised and Gun-shy.

Step 1: Complete the "Bruised and Gun-shy" Self-Assessments

A recurring theme and recommended first step in this book is to know yourself first before you reach out to the external world. If you know your preferences, your values, and your parameters, you will find it easier to understand your needs and boundaries in a work situation. For example, if stability, security, affiliation, and a regular paycheck are important to you, starting a business or working as a free agent may not be the most advisable choices for you to pursue. First, review the results of the values, attitudes, and change readiness self-assessments you completed earlier in chapter 3, on pages 31, 35–36, and 39–40. By doing this, you will have a better chance of identifying the best job for you and avoiding another unpleasant work situation.

It makes sense to reflect on your past work situation to help you assess what you'll need and want in your future work. Using the results of the self-assessments you just reviewed, think about the specific work situation that was difficult or painful for you and answer the following questions.

VALUES

Were my values truly being met in that particular work situation?

_____

_____

Which ones were?

_____

_____

_____

Which values were not?

_____

_____

_____

ATTITUDES

Look back at the job or work situation that caused you to feel Bruised and Gun-shy and assess what you have learned about your attitudes.

_____

_____

_____

_____

_____

_____

SELF-CONFIDENCE

Has your self-confidence eroded? If it has, focus on using one of your strengths or skills to help in regaining your confidence.

If you're working now, is there a task or project you can complete or a goal you can reach that will help you feel good about yourself as well as give you recognition? If you aren't working currently, can you find a consulting job in which you can use your technical expertise to help a client solve a problem? Write down your ideas.

_____

_____

_____

_____

SELF-KNOWLEDGE

Did you learn something new about yourself during your difficult situation that you weren't previously aware of? Did you receive feedback about a specific behavior or skill? Be honest with yourself. Write down what it is along with three ways that you can change or improve it (take a class, identify a mentor, buy a self-help audiotape).

_____

_____

_____

_____

MANAGING RELATIONSHIPS

Did you experience friction or discord with a specific person during your difficult work experience? While some people are truly tough to deal with in the workplace, a relationship involves two people, not just one. What did you learn about the way you handle relationships from your negative experience? If you became involved in a difficult relationship at work again, what would you do differently?

_____

_____

_____

_____

MAINTAINING MOTIVATION

Do you feel focused and energetic about your career? Does the work you've been involved with still interest and stimulate you? If not, write down three to five activities that you can become involved with to increase your motivation overall. Some suggestions are increasing your exercise routine, taking an art class, researching a new industry, and volunteering for a social cause.

_____

_____

_____

_____

GOAL ORIENTATION

Setting goals is an important part of making changes. Regardless of how severe your Bruised and Gun-shy state is, you must set goals for yourself and your career. Write down two goals that will help you to move toward a more optimistic frame of mind. Examples: Completing all of the assessments in this book and spending two hours a week researching a new career.

_____

_____

_____

_____

PROFESSIONAL COMMITMENT

Do you feel completely committed to your job and your career? If not, is it because you feel battered by your recent negative work experience or because you no longer have passion or interest for your career? Write down the things you can do to regain the professional commitment you once had.

CHANGE READINESS

Refer to the results of your self-assessment on handling change on pages 39–40. If you are Bruised and Gun-shy, it is likely that your score may reflect this by indicating that you are not comfortable making changes. Identify two positive changes related to work that you can make today or tomorrow that will help you move away from being Bruised and Gun-shy.

INTERESTS

When you think about the work situation that left you feeling Bruised and Gun-shy, how did you feel about the actual work itself? Was the work you were doing interesting to you? If so, what about it interested you?

Were there aspects of your job that did not interest you? If so, what were they? Describe why.

Step 2: Explore Roadblocks and Opportunities

Once you've determined that you are healing and are more readily equipped to decide what kind of work situation is right for you, it's time to prepare yourself if you inadvertently walk into another difficult situation. While this may seem to be a negative approach, the truth is that the likelihood of your being laid off, caught in a merger, or accepting a job with a company whose culture isn't a fit for you is very strong. Even if you decide to start your own business or work as a contractor, there's no guarantee that you will experience success. You are, after all, human, and many forces affect your work that you cannot control.

Rupert, a general manager in consumer products, has had a successful career with several very difficult patches along the way. While he does admit to being Bruised and Gun-shy, he also says that he has learned how to deal with the arduous times in his career that he knows will occur again. In his last position, he worked for someone who admitted to Rupert in his first interview that his nickname was the "Yale Terminator." Unfortunately, Rupert ignored this obvious sign that his prospective boss was cruel and took the job anyway because it was a challenging, international opportunity. When he left his position, he said that he felt he was in physical danger from his boss. What is Rupert's advice? "Separate what was about you and what was about the other person. Hang on to the fundamental realization that nothing will last forever. Take the position and the set of work for what it's worth. No matter what you were promised when you were hired, accept it, as that's as good as it gets. Manage your expectations." He adds, "You lose a certain elasticity as you move along in your career and you need to have something to fall back on. Have a support group. For me, it's my wife and my kids."

Usually, when people interview for a new job they look at the job title, location, work responsibilities, and compensation first. Although these factors are all important, they are rarely the reason a job doesn't work out. Instead, the three primary reasons are your boss, the company culture, or that the job has been misrepresented or changes once you're in it. You can help avoid these problems by doing the following three things before you accept a new job.

1. Assess Your Prospective Boss

Bill DeLeno, a psychotherapist in private practice in White Plains, New York, specializes in helping people with problems at work. He asserts that the number-one difficulty that people have at work is their boss. One of Bill's patients actually told him that he was so afraid of his boss he couldn't go to his mother's funeral because he had to work.

Not everyone is as obvious as Rupert's new boss, who admitted up front to Rupert what his horrifying nickname was. If you've had a bad experience with a boss, then you will naturally try to learn as much as you can about the person you'll report to in your next job. Even so, few people feel comfortable "interviewing" their possible future boss. Instead, we behave as if the relationship goes one way instead of two. It's important to keep in mind that this person is crucial to your success or failure in your job, so the more you can find out about your prospective new boss before you start working for him or her, the better off you'll be. Remember that bosses usually show their "best face" to you during the interviewing process, especially if they see you as a viable candidate for the job they're trying to fill. If your prospective boss is rude, insensitive, or appears uninterested in you during the interview, this behavior will only become magnified during your working relationship. Asking the following questions will help uncover his or her personality quirks and style:

How would you describe the ideal relationship you could have with someone who reports to you?

What would you expect of me during my first three months at this job? First six months? First year?

How does this align with the organization's expectations? What about its strategy?

What about your job keeps you up at night? How would I help you with the solution to this challenge?

How do you like to communicate and receive information from the people who report to you? How often?

How would you describe your work style?

What should I realistically expect from you as my manager?

Who was the best boss you ever had and why?

What are your top three values?

How do you think people view you within the organization?

Some of these are tough questions to ask; however, an individual's willingness to answer the questions and his or her candor in doing so can be very telling. When you ask any or all of these questions, do so in a very nonthreatening way so that your prospective boss isn't turned off.

The most useful information you can get about your prospective boss is from the people who presently work for him or her or have done so in the past. Why is it okay for the people interviewing you to ask you whatever they are legally allowed to and it isn't okay for you? It's not right! Working involves a mutual agreement. Your response to the question: "Why do you want to talk with these people?" is the following: "I want a productive relationship that is going to be the best possible fit for both of us. I know what it costs to recruit, hire, and retain an employee, financially and psychologically."

Whoever you question may be cautious about answering, particularly when the answers may not be positive. Again, be sensitive to their position of needing to protect themselves and their job. Read between the lines and probe.

When you are speaking to someone who currently works for or has reported in the past to your prospective boss, ask these questions:

How would you describe your relationship with him?

What are his strengths? What about areas that need development?

How is he viewed within the organization? Why?

Who is he close to in the organization?

Does he make decisions? Does he involve you in those decisions?

How does he like to be communicated with (regular meetings, in the hallway, e-mail, reports, voice mail)?

How would you describe his work style?

Does he give feedback? How and when?

What characteristics does he admire?

Does he value and support work/life balance?

How does he deal with conflict?

What are his priorities in his job?

What are his hot buttons or pet peeves?

If he hires me, what advice would you give me to ensure that we get started on the right foot together?

You'll notice that some of these questions are the same as the ones you've asked your prospective boss. Pay attention to how many of the answers are the same or similar and which are not.

If your prospective boss is new to the organization, ask him if you can speak to someone at his previous job. Again, if he balks, be concerned.

With the constant change that occurs within organizations, you may not be working for the same person for very long. We all know, however, that even three months of working for someone with whom we don't get along can feel like an eternity!

2. Assess the Company's Culture

Every work environment has its own culture. If you fit into a company's culture—the values employees share, the way people communicate and dress, the behaviors that are accepted—then you probably will have a good working experience. On the other hand, if you don't fit in, regardless of how talented you are at your job or what you've accomplished, the chances are strong that you will either derail voluntarily or you will be asked to leave the organization.

A company's culture is very powerful and cannot be changed by one person, even a new leader, overnight. A culture is an interwoven system of beliefs, values, history, mythology, rituals, and ceremonies. In a work context, these create meaning for people, and although it may not always be easy to describe it to others outside the organization, the company culture definitely influences behavior and the way business is conducted.

Because of this, it is important that you learn how to effectively assess a company's culture to determine if it is a fit for you. Remember, you spend a lot of time working. There is no reason to be unhappy or to be working in an unsuitable work situation. If you've already had an experience in which you went to work for a company and realized you didn't fit into the culture, you know how painful this can be. Learning how to identify the right culture for you is easy to do if you ask the right questions and rely on your intuition.

Several elements of company culture are important to consider when you are pursuing a new opportunity. One important element is that of values and beliefs. Values and beliefs are principles, standards, or qualities considered inherently worthwhile and desirable. They cannot always be neatly defined in a manual. Values create focus and shape behavior. An historic person in the company (a past leader or pioneer) exemplifies core values and beliefs. Now that you have identified your own top-ten values, it will be easier to ask questions in an interview to find out how closely your values match those of your prospective employer.

Think about what you want in a company culture from a "clean slate" perspective, especially if you have never felt as if you fit into a company culture in the past or have had some disappointments. Sit at your computer or take a piece of paper and list the ideal elements that you want and need to feel comfortable in your work environment. Forget about reality for the moment. You can go back to your list later and focus on what you think is realistic.

How do you assess a company's culture? By asking lots of questions; meeting as many people as you can; sitting in the parking lot and observing; sitting in the reception area; looking at the company's Web site, marketing materials, and annual report; and—*most important*—by following your intuition. As a prospective employee, you have every right to talk to as many people as you need to, including vendors, clients, and employees who don't work in your functional area. If there is resistance to this, take note and be wary. Remember, if your gut is telling you that something is not quite right, in all likelihood, it isn't! It's okay to be excited or interested in a particular job opportunity but don't fixate on the title, money, perks, or job description and lose sight of the one aspect of the job that can make or break your chances of success—the culture!

At the same time, a word of caution—"fit" means the most suitable. You will not find perfection in any job or work situation because it does not exist. Companies are not always completely candid about their cultures. This is another reason to try to talk with as many different people as possible before signing on.

Here are some questions you can ask to assess a company's culture:

How would you describe the culture here?

What is important to senior management here?

How are decisions made? (By senior management only, by consensus, collaboratively, by crisis, or not at all?)

What is the typical background of the people here?

How important is the customer or client?

What kind of hierarchy exists in the company?

What is the preferred method of communication (e-mail, memos, meetings, voice mail, or impromptu hallway conversations)?

Is feedback valued? Does it occur and in what form?

Is innovation or risk-taking valued and rewarded?

How often, when, and why do people leave the company? (Of their own volition, are people fired?)

Who are some of the successful people in the company and why?

Psychotherapist Bill DeLeno advises that even if you've done a thorough job of assessing a company, "You don't know what you've got until you get there." While it's not easy advice to follow, Bill recommends that if you do find yourself in a situation that is making you very unhappy and you can't seem to change it, "don't linger if it's bad. Every job and work experience is a stepping stone today, anyway."

3. Assess the Job Itself

When you are interviewing for a new job, it is normal to ask questions about the responsibilities you'll have. It's also important to ask questions about the business goals you'll be expected to achieve. Whether you are starting a new job with a company or moving into a new role with your current employer, ask these questions of your boss:

Why does this job exist?

What are your expectations of me in my first three months in this position?

How will you measure my success after a year in this job?

How does this job fit within the department or division?

Who worked in this job before and where did he or she go?

What did he or she accomplish in this job?

What was difficult for him or her?

What do you think my greatest challenge will be in this job?

What are my top three most important business priorities in this job?

Whenever you start a new job or are promoted, create a plan with your new boss and any other stakeholders (stakeholders include peers, direct reports, and senior management) who can influence your work and job.

Jackie got a big promotion to run operations for the sales division of her company. Jackie was an assistant controller with no experience in sales; when she was asked what her plans were for her first thirty, sixty, and ninety days, it hadn't even occurred to Jackie that she should have a plan. Not only did she need to understand what her boss was interested in accomplishing, but she was also inheriting a big staff. The first thing she should have done was to make an appointment with her new boss and prepare a list of questions for him. She then should have scheduled a one-on-one meeting with every single person on her staff to get to know them individually, and understand what they had contributed in the past as well as what they would like to do moving forward. Jackie needed to make a strong first impression to everyone in her new role because the department was experiencing problems and because initially Jackie wouldn't have seemed an obvious choice for the job.

Once Jackie gathered all this information and started to develop relationships, she needed to set goals that were measurable and realistic, and have her boss and any other stakeholders sign off on them. Going forward, Jackie should meet with everyone at least every forty-five to sixty days. If possible, she should make an ally out of the person who was previously in her role.

It's just as important to continue assessing your job once you've been doing it for a while. While most people who are laid off from their jobs aren't fired because of performance, people do lose their jobs because business priorities shift. With this shift comes the assumption that different skills may be needed. Most companies aren't very good at assessing their employees' skills and putting them in a different role that will benefit both employees and their company. Often a person is hired to accomplish one thing, and if the needs of the organization change, that person may no longer be viewed as relevant to the company's new priorities. Sometimes it's difficult to know whether you are still viewed as integral to the company's priorities. How can you be aware of this in your company, so that you aren't caught off guard? Unfortunately, very few people are aware that they may be losing their job when they actually do. Sadly, very few people take care of the things that they can control before they lose their job. As a result, the recovery period takes much longer.

What can you do to stay aware of the status of your job? In *Are You a Corporate Refugee?*, Ruth Luban talks about the "signposts" that signify the first phase of being a corporate refugee, what she calls "On the Brink," when you know something is amiss at your company. Some of the signposts that Luban describes in her book are things like: frequent reorganizations; budget cuts; vacancies left unfulfilled; you're not being invited to the planning meetings you always used to attend; a boss who doesn't have time to meet with you; a merger or buyout of your company.

Instead of burying your head in the sand to avoid what you think may be happening, Luban recommends some things you can do to replace your feelings of uncertainty with structure. She suggests that engaging in these practical activities will equip you for the possibility that the signposts are indeed leading to the loss of your job. Here are some of her recommendations:

Start networking with recruiters, your competition, former colleagues, and trade associations.

Get organized by cleaning out your desk files, your computer files, and updating your Rolodex.

Use your benefits by scheduling all those doctors' appointments you've been putting off. Staying healthy is more important than ever while you're going through this stressful time.

Simplify your life by reducing clutter and winnowing down scheduled activities.

Reorganize your finances by assessing your savings and looking at areas where you can cut expenses; avoid using credit cards.

Taking action in these areas will help you feel more in control and less stressed in the event that you do lose your job.

Step 3: Create an Action Plan

Now that you've looked at what you learned from your past work experiences, and determined what you want from your next job, it is important to create a plan to move ahead.

Answer the following questions:

What do you want your work to look like in three months? Six months? A year? Describe it as specifically as you can.

Three months

_____

_____

_____

Six months

_____

_____

_____

A year

_____

_____

_____

What steps do you need to take to make this happen? What kind of research should you do? What resources do you need to move forward?

Steps to take (update your résumé, set up meetings with your network, have a conversation with your current boss):

_____

_____

_____

_____

Research to do (learn about a new industry, interview several people who are working in a job that you'd like to do):

_____

_____

_____

_____

Resources you need (buy a new computer, find a mentor):

_____

_____

_____

_____

Do you want to be on your own? If this is the route you think you'd like to take, it is even more important to recover from feeling Bruised and Gun-shy because planning and starting a new business will tap all of your energy and many of your resources.

———

Pat was a managing counsel for a major commercial bank. She had a great job, but had been doing it for twenty years. She stayed because she liked the work and it was near her home and two children. But then the bank began to sell off assets in her area. Pat was downsized two weeks before she turned fifty. "I was traumatized at first and started looking for a job with another large financial company, although everyone told me that I should be in my own business. I took some private clients during my job search. I loved it and decided to go into business for myself. That's a very risky thing to do at my age, since I need to maintain a certain income level and my husband is not making a lot. But it's turned out to be a very rewarding second career."

Ask yourself the following questions:

If you want to be on your own, what kind of work do you want to do?

_____

_____

_____

_____

How will you begin the process of planning your own business?
(Read chapter 9, "Yearning to Be on Your Own" first!)

_____

_____

_____

_____

How will you manage stress and maintain your psychological
well-being (take yoga classes, write in your journal, spend extra
time with your family)?

_____

_____

_____

_____

Before she was fired, Susie worked in sales. Her employer and
another larger company merged and she was let go for "political" reasons. "I stayed a year longer than I should have," Susie
admits, "because I was determined to make it work." Her counsel to others? "Remember who you are. Remember what successes you've had in the past. Don't let anyone strip away your
self-confidence. Stay whole."

List three successes you've had in your career that you are especially proud of:

_____

_____

Whatever your current and future work choices are for yourself—staying in your present job, changing careers, starting a business or retiring—think of what you've learned from the difficult working situations you may have experienced. Use these lessons to be more prepared to deal with losing your job, working for a difficult boss, or experiencing a merger. While much of what has happened to you in the past may have been out of your control, if you are clear about what you need and can tolerate in your next work situation, you will feel more in control if you get involved in another difficult situation.

CHAPTER 8

Bored and Plateaued

Most of us have felt bored or unchallenged at some point in our lives, whether for a few hours, several months, or even years at a time. If you've been involved in the same kind of work for a while, you've probably reached the top of your game from a competency standpoint. It feels good to be viewed by your professional peers, friends, and family as an expert in your field. Chances are you also enjoy many perks, including healthy compensation, status, and the overall feeling of having "made it" in your career.

But the picture might not be completely rosy. You may be so comfortable that you have begun to feel plateaued, which is to say, stifled, unchallenged, or bored. Not only do you feel listless, restless, aimless, or disengaged with the tasks you're performing or the people you work with, but you also exhibit "bored" behaviors. These behaviors including making a lot of personal calls and sending tons of e-mail to your friends, taking at least a half-dozen coffee and food breaks, and fantasizing about becoming the next million-dollar lottery winner and telling your boss that you're quitting your job. When you're bored and your coworkers don't seem to be bored, you naturally feel alienated and weird.

Feeling bored or plateaued can occur gradually so that you are able to shrug it off for a time, or it may come on suddenly and linger chronically so that it isn't quite as easy to ignore. If you are feeling bored, you may not necessarily be feeling plateaued. If you are experiencing one of these feelings, however, you are probably susceptible to the other as well.

Being bored or plateaued does not mean that you aren't working hard or that you don't have enough work to do. Being busy and dealing with the excessive stimulation that the workplace provides us with today have little to do with being bored. The combination of the two merely leads to a greater level of burnout.

Through more than ten years of conducting career development workshops, Kurt Sandholtz of BT Novations, a national career management consulting firm that works with companies to help their employees learn to take charge of their own growth and development, has gathered extensive data on why and how people become Bored and Plateaued. He explains that most people typically pass through three phases during the course of their careers: phase 1—low skill and high passion; phase 2—high passion and high skill; phase 3—high skill and low passion. Sandholtz's phase 3 is a great shorthand description for Bored and Plateaued. Although being Bored and Plateaued is more likely to happen to someone who is more senior in their career, it can happen at any age.

Psychologist Judith Bardwick, author of *The Plateauing Trap: How to Avoid It in Your Career and in Your Life*, uses the phrase "structural plateauing" to describe the end of promotions and "content plateauing" to depict the end of growth and learning. Similarly, Kurt Sandholtz labels these two types of plateauing as position plateauing and contribution plateauing. Regardless of what terms we use to describe it, the reality is that corporations today are unable to offer the kinds of promotional opportunities they could fifteen or twenty years ago. This is a reflection of both corporate downsizing and a gradual elimination of the promotional ladder. Many of us already have and will continue to experience this corporate "ceiling," while all of us can face, as Sandholtz points out, the end of promotions, which naturally occurs eventually in a career.

When you were promoted in the past, you knew that with that promotion would come new experiences, different relationships, and the opportunity to develop new skills. If you have been in the same job for several years, or haven't learned anything new for a while, it's easy to become stifled by repetition and disinterested in the overfamiliar tasks you routinely perform. Although it's normal for a productive person to experience such feelings on occasion, there are many negative ramifications of being in this predicament, particularly long-term. For one thing, it becomes increasingly difficult to hide your feelings from your boss, peers, subordinates, and clients. Rachelle, a senior human resources director, recalls being pulled aside by her boss and asked if she wanted to take some extended time off because she didn't seem engaged in her work the way she used to be. She expressed surprise that her boss had picked up on her boredom so easily.

If you've been in the same job for a while, without the benefit of ongoing continuing education opportunities, your skills may become outdated and you could become viewed by others as someone who is no longer "state-of-the-art." Over and over again, research has shown that the healthiest, most productive adult is the one who is constantly learning and growing, not the one who is stagnant.

Working in a job or career where you are Bored and Plateaued can produce many negative emotional, psychological, and physical effects. Feeling depressed, anxious, unmotivated, or frustrated not only affects your work, but also quickly impacts the rest of your life, including your significant relationships and even your health.

Barbara, a senior financial analyst who is forty years old, has been in the same role for three years and is so bored with her job that she thinks of reasons not to go to work. Her boredom at work has also eroded the quality of her personal life. Barbara, who is single, isn't interested in going on vacation, and feels so boring that she can't imagine why anyone would date her. She's gradually gained weight during the last several years and isn't doing anything to lose it. Barbara is so plateaued in her life that she is simply waiting for someone or something to motivate her to make the changes she knows she needs to make.

If you like your field or aspects of the work you do but have mastered the essentials and are hungry to learn new things, you are probably Bored and Plateaued. It's time to learn what you can do to change your feelings from Bored and Plateaued to committed, creative, competent, and energized. Remember also that many people feel bored or stifled at some point in their career, so it's important to analyze your situation carefully and identify the culprit—what's really boring you—before taking action to eliminate these feelings.

Step 1: Complete the "Bored and Plateaued" Self-Assessment

Flip back to the self-assessments you took on interests on pages 48–53 and favorite skills on pages 54–57. Review your responses.

Now it's time to look at your current work situation. Answer the following questions below. Your goal here is to identify your interests and favorite skills that are being satisfied in your job currently and to think of ways to eliminate some of the things that are causing you to feel Bored and Plateaued.

1. How would you describe what you do for a living? Avoid using a title of any kind.

_____

_____

_____

_____

2. Which of your favorite skills do you use most frequently in your current position? (Refer to your list of favorite skills in chapter 4.)

_____

_____

_____

_____

3. What do you like the most about your job (tangible or intangible)?

_____

_____

_____

_____

4. How could you augment this aspect of your job? Be specific.

_____

_____

_____

5. What do you like least about your job (tangible or intangible)?

_____

_____

_____

_____

6. Can you find a way to reduce or eliminate this aspect? If so, describe how.

_____

_____

_____

_____

7. Describe your feelings of boredom.

_____

_____

_____

8. Describe why you feel plateaued.

_____

_____

_____

9. Do you currently have any specific career goals? If so, what are they?

_____

_____

_____

_____

10. What do you believe are the obstacles preventing you from moving out of your Bored and Plateaued situation?

_____

_____

_____

_____

11. What could help you move into a fulfilling and rewarding work situation?

_____

_____

_____

_____

Answering these basic questions should help you to understand your current work situation more clearly. You will refer to your answers later.

Step 2: Explore Roadblocks and Opportunities

Wanda was a forty-year-old vice president of marketing in the consumer products industry who was "bored silly" and felt stuck in her job. She was unchallenged, not using her strengths, and, because she had been in this Bored and Plateaued phase for several years, she was not motivated to make a career change, though she desperately wanted to. Wanda dreamed of being an interior designer or working in the fashion industry.

When Wanda finally began to do something about her feelings, she took a series of assessments, which revealed that she is extroverted, intuitive, makes decisions based upon her values, and prefers spontaneity. Her primary values are creativity and autonomy. A typical baby boomer, she is concerned about earning less money than she does now, and, because she hasn't saved much, she isn't willing to decrease her compensation dramatically. She is single, and although she works hard when challenged, she is very interested in attaining a balanced lifestyle. Since she estimates that she will have to work for another twenty-five years, Wanda wants to move into a field that offers a variety of opportunities for her to work flexibly and long-term.

When Wanda answered the questions listed on pages 125 to 128, she discovered that the chances were slim that she would ever muster the interest or energy to change something about her current job to alleviate her boredom. The truth is, although she knew her business well and was very comfortable, she just couldn't bring herself to think of ways to revitalize her situation to make it work for her. She yearned to leave consumer products marketing. Fortunately, she knew that she was interested in the interior design and fashion fields. She was also pretty clear about what her skills were—in the areas of marketing, operations, and working with clients. Because she was certain that just changing her current situation wouldn't alleviate her boredom, and was clear about wanting to move out of her field altogether, she was faced with the prospect of changing careers. Wanda's first obstacle was believing that it was actually possible for her to switch fields without taking a significant cut in pay. She was especially worried about having to accept an entry-level position with an entry-level salary. Initially, this fear slowed her down. Like many prospective career-changers, Wanda put obstacles in her own way to mask her fear of the unknown. In his book *The Pathfinder,* Nicholas Lore calls these manufactured obstacles "Yeahbuts." He lists twenty-five or so, including: "I don't have enough talent," "I'm too young/too stupid," "I'm not committed enough," "I'm over/under educated," "I'm over/under qualified," "I have too much/too little experience."

Yet, once Wanda had made up her mind that changing fields was what she was going to do, her entire attitude shifted and she felt excited about her next career. She began brainstorming ways to meet people in the interior design and fashion industries so that she could learn more about the kinds of opportunities that might exist for her. Wanda started networking with people in her two target industries. She didn't spend a lot of time doing it, but every week she would talk on the phone or meet with someone in interior design or fashion. As she became immersed in this process, her excitement grew, confirming that she was correct in her original assessment that she should be working in fashion or interior design. Interestingly, once Wanda found the motivation to change careers, she wasn't nearly as focused on the issue of compensation.

Every once in a while, Wanda's energy flagged and she would stop networking. When this happened, she would identify one simple action step to reignite the spark, which would help her feel motivated once again. Then, after three months, Wanda ran into Ursula, a friend from high school, and, as she did with everyone, told her what she was trying to do. Her friend reminded Wanda that another mutual friend, Cynthia, whom Wanda hadn't seen in a long time, owned an agency for designers in New York City. Wanda met with Cynthia, who gave her several names of people to phone in the design industry. Wanda started calling them. Not long afterward, she heard from Cynthia, who asked if she would be interested in running sales for her business, since the person in that position was going on maternity leave and not planning to return. Wanda jumped at the opportunity and has been happily working for Cynthia for nearly two years. She feels incredibly fulfilled, and—the icing on the cake—is making exactly the same salary she was earning in her former career!

Wanda is an example of someone who changed her Bored and Plateaued status by leaving her job and her industry. The first thing you should do if you are feeling Bored and Plateaued is take a look at your current situation.

Favorite Skills

How did you respond to the question "What favorite skills do you use the most frequently?" Whatever favorite skills you identified, would you feel more engaged and interested if you could increase the time you spent using these? If you like to write but really only write business memos and e-mail messages, is there a way to increase the amount of writing you do by starting a division newsletter or approaching your local newspaper to write a monthly column?

Take a look at the favorite skills you wrote down on page 56 and think of different opportunities you could create to make them a bigger part of your work life. Write down every possible opportunity you come up with. For the moment, forget about any obstacles you perceive that could prevent you from making it happen.

_____

_____

_____

_____

_____

_____

_____

Tasks

Take a look at your list of things you least enjoy in your work from pages 126–27. Doing tasks that we don't enjoy can lead to boredom and ultimately to unhappiness. Put on your creative hat and think of ways to get these tasks off your plate. Is there someone to whom you could delegate them—an intern, assistant, junior staff member, outside vendor, or peer—who enjoys that type of work more than you do? If you could eliminate or reduce these tasks you don't enjoy, and spend your time doing other things, would you be less bored? Write them down along with ideas for delegating or eliminating them.

_____

_____

_____

_____

Remember when you weren't bored?

Can you think back and recall when you began to feel bored in your work? Did boredom creep up on you slowly or was it triggered by a specific incident or situation? Write down how you think it would feel if you were no longer bored in your work. Can you even imagine what that would feel like? If you can't, then look back on your career and try to recall a time when you felt energized and challenged. How was your situation then different from the situation you're in now?

_____

_____

_____

_____

_____

Revitalizing your current situation

Despite being Bored and Plateaued, you may decide to stay with your current employer for a year or two more, or you may not. If you're leaning toward leaving your present job, before you do, make sure you have explored what you could change in your current job situation that could alleviate your current state.

How? First, be clear about what you'd like to change before you approach other people in your organization. Also, be sure that you are able to communicate what the benefit is to your employer. Let's take Rachelle's situation, mentioned earlier. Rachelle's boss had asked her if she wanted to take time off because she seemed bored and disinterested in her work. Rachelle grabbed the opportunity. After taking three weeks off and traveling, Rachelle realized that she really loved human resources and just needed a new challenge. Although she did begin to conduct a job search outside her company, Rachelle, who loves to travel, ended up interviewing for and accepting a human resources director position for her current employer, in which she provides support for the company's Latin American division. In her new job, she works in a function she loves, but with a much greater degree of autonomy. She feels energized and stimulated, quite different from the way she felt just six months before she started her new position.

Rachelle is fortunate that she works for a company large enough to provide internal job opportunities for its employees. Her employer realized that Rachelle, a talented HR professional with exceptional people skills and an understanding of the complex political workings of the organization, was an asset to the company and an employee worth keeping.

Even if you work for a smaller company, if you and your employer are creative, you will find many ways to create an exciting new job description to add new and different responsibilities to your current job. Most Bored and Plateaued people immediately think about leaving their company rather than finding a way to change their present work situation. But leaving isn't always the answer. If your employer values you, then it is in his or her best interest to keep you and to help you find a way to reenergize yourself, for the benefit of the organization. If not, there is a company out there that *will* appreciate you.

Changing the dynamics of your job may or may not be the solution to your Bored and Plateaued state. Learning something new can be an effective hedge against boredom, but those familiar feelings may return once you've mastered a new skill or successfully taken on a new challenge. That's why it's so critical to analyze the source of your Bored and Plateaued feelings before applying what could turn out to be a mere Band-Aid solution.

Staying in your industry

If you have investigated changing your work or moving into a new position at your current company but there are real obstacles to making this happen or you really don't want to change careers right now, there are several other options you can explore. The most obvious is to find a new position in your current industry—either the same type of job you have now or a different role in another company. Be cautious about using this tactic. Consider the case of Donna. She worked as a human resource generalist for a publishing company. After six years, she was bored, but decided to "hang in" because of rumors of an impending takeover of her company by another publishing house. Sure enough, this occurred, and Donna received a nice severance package. After taking the summer off, Donna started her job search. Results from assessments and feedback from several friends helped Donna discover that she had the ideal personality for sales. Although sales sounded appealing to Donna, the thought of leaving HR and taking a risk made her nervous, so she accepted the first offer she got—as an HR generalist at a relocation company. Unfortunately, it was a bad fit. Donna couldn't relate to the employees and was uncomfortable with the way they communicated, along with many other aspects of the company culture. She decided to quit without having another job and worked as a temporary recruiter for six months. Again, she conducted a job search and, ignoring the voice in her head and her friends' advice, accepted yet another HR generalist position, back in the publishing industry. Although this time the firm's culture is comfortable for Donna, she is back where she was almost two years ago. She is still sitting at her desk, thinking about how to find the courage to leave human resources and go into sales. Unfortunately, Donna is plagued with doubts and keeps hearing the message she received growing up: find a good job with a decent salary and stick with it, through thick or thin.

David is another example of someone who is bored and plateaued. He had been in the entertainment industry for ten years and he was bored. At the beginning of each new job (he has had three), he wasn't at all bored, because he had to adjust to a different culture, get to know new players, and learn new skills. When he really explored the root of his boredom, however, David discovered that throughout his career he'd been using a lot of skills that he really wasn't interested in using, and wasn't using others that he loved. David determined that he wanted to write more, develop creative messages or promotional campaigns, and function in a more persuasive role. He also had a deep interest in current affairs, politics, and media. David created a list of favorite skills that he wanted to be using every day: identifying public affairs, public relations, and media consulting as avenues to explore. Once he identified these new areas, he felt excited and very committed.

Changing jobs in your industry makes sense if you love the industry and haven't yet accomplished the things you'd like to accomplish or learned everything you could. It also makes sense if you're unable to move into a role that interests you within your current company. If this is what you want, be very focused and adamant about communicating to prospective employers in your industry that you will only move if you are given a different role than the one you currently have. Otherwise, it's likely that you'll be bored after six months to a year, and back to where you were before you changed jobs.

Focusing on the world outside of work

Another solution to overcoming boredom or lack of learning in your work is to focus your energy on the world outside of your job. As adults, we all have interests or untapped talents that we've allowed to fade because of our work and family responsibilities. Take a look at the results of your interests self-assessment and select one thing that jumps out at you. Plan to take a class, hire a coach, or attend a workshop. It's not recommended that you ignore your Bored and Plateaued state at work indefinitely, but revitalizing yourself in another area of your life can energize your personal life now and your career later on.

By engaging yourself in something that you find fun, exciting, interesting, or fulfilling, you may discover the key to ending boredom in your career. You also may learn how to weave your outside interests into your work. This can be accomplished in several ways.

One option is to involve yourself intensively in your interest outside of work, while working your "day job" to satisfy your need to earn a living. Robert is an example. An avid foxhunter who owns two horses, he spends nearly every waking moment of his spare time either foxhunting or socializing with other foxhunters. During the week, however, he puts business clothes on and drives into Atlanta to his job as a contingency recruiter for an agency. While he doesn't particularly like his job, he earns a good living, which allows him to support his expensive outside interest. This is an easy trade-off for him to make, since his enjoyment of foxhunting far outweighs the boredom he feels at his job.

Another option is to do as Julia did—eventually find a way to turn your passion into a full-time job. For eight years, Julia did speaking engagements on topics like sales, networking, and career management for local associations for free, simply because she enjoyed giving talks. Every year, the number of speeches she gave increased. Several years ago, when she was at a crossroads in her sales career, she was having lunch with an acquaintance who commented that Julia lit up when she talked about public speaking. That moment changed Julia's life. Soon after that lunch, she began to make plans to speak professionally. It honestly had never occurred to her that public speaking was what she should do for a living. Until that moment, Julia simply thought of it as a fun hobby.

Turning an avocation into a vocation can be a scary proposition; doing it successfully requires planning that includes preparing yourself psychologically and financially. After that fateful lunch, Julia spent eight months working in a transitional job she disliked while planning and priming herself to start her professional speaking practice. As stressful as Julia's "for the time being" job was, the income and structure it offered made her transition much smoother and less frightening.

If you can't shake the feeling that "it just isn't fun anymore," as Kurt Sandholtz says, because you're stuck in phase 3—high skill, low passion—now is the time to realize it, accept it, and start moving forward. Start small by learning something new or, as Sandholtz suggests, start looking at your job from the outside in and think about how you can approach it differently. And if that doesn't nip your boredom in the bud, start the exhilarating process of changing your career.

Step 3: Create an Action Plan

As you figure out how you intend to eliminate your Bored and Plateaued situation, you need to have clear answers to the following questions.

What are the reasons for your boredom with work?

_____

_____

_____

_____

How can you revitalize or change your current job or working situation so that you won't be bored?

_____

_____

_____

_____

Do you want to pursue a different job within your industry? If so, how will you do this?

_____

_____

_____

_____

List the reasons why you would accept another job in your industry.

_____

_____

_____

_____

Have you decided to change careers and leave your industry? If so, write down what steps you will take in the following four areas:

Self-assessment

_____

_____

_____

_____

Research

_____

_____

_____

_____

Writing your résumé

_____

_____

_____

_____

Networking to learn about the industry you're interested in and uncover job openings.

_____

_____

_____

_____

Do you have a hobby or interest that you'd like to spend more time with? If so, what do you need to do to make this happen?

_____

_____

_____

_____

Regardless of what you decide to do first, it's important that you do something—anything—to begin to alleviate your feeling of boredom. Use your Bored and Plateaued state as a launchpad to new and satisfying work. The choice is yours.

CHAPTER 9

Yearning to Be on Your Own

If you're dreaming of starting your own business, you are not alone. A survey conducted by the accounting firm Ernst & Young found that 78 percent of influential Americans believe that entrepreneurship will be the defining trend of the twenty-first century. Why is this so? The study identified six factors as the primary reasons that a growing number of people are thinking about, planning, and starting their own businesses:

1. Technology
2. Economic conditions
3. Social conditions
4. Advent of the global economy
5. Government deregulation
6. Inability of large corporations to innovate

A study of entrepreneurism by the American Society for Training and Development (ASTD) stated, "There is a huge emphasis on entrepreneurial training as an economic development issue, particularly in rural and high unemployment areas. Colleges are now adding more training in this area." The study concluded, "Entrepreneurism will continue. One trend is in two-income families. Often one partner will take a 'regular' corporate job, while the other pursues an entreprenurial start-up. The latter will become their future. Technology is making it much easier for entrepreneurs to flourish."

The number of people thinking about or already working in their own business is also increasing across demographic groups. According to *The Futurist* magazine, baby boomers (those born between 1946 and 1964), considered to be the healthiest and most educated generation in history, will start retiring from their traditional careers and a large number will start their own businesses.

Gen Xers (the generation born after the boomers, between 1965 and 1978) are also naturally more entrepreneurial in spirit, and they, too, won't hesitate to start their own busi-nesses. Gen Xers don't tend to view starting a business as a risky venture, the way many baby boomers may have. This lack of skepticism toward entrepreneurism is even truer of individ-uals who are younger than Gen Xers. In 1999, *Business Week* published a survey that found that 65 percent of fourteen- to nineteen-year-olds (Millennials) say they're interested in start-ing a business.

In 2001, there were 8 million privately owned businesses in the United States alone. If you are thinking about starting your own business, what is motivating you to do so? You've heard the cliché "You can be your own boss" touted as the overriding benefit of "running your own show." It's true—you have no one to hold accountable but yourself for what you either achieve or fail to achieve in your own business.

Consider these other reasons:

Catherine, an independent contractor who handles market-ing for a catalog company, says, "I like the freedom that comes from working for myself."

Leonard, an author, journalist, and psychotherapist who earned his master's degree in counseling at age fifty-two, says,

"I am on my own and am quite aware of the drawbacks, such as a lack of resources and a lonely feeling at times. But I get more of a sense of meaning from my work by being on my own."

Barri worked as a chief operating officer of a $12 million start-up company and became ill. She left, took a four-year sabbatical, and then tried to go back to work at a *Fortune* 500 company. "I knew it was a mistake almost the day I started." Now, says Barri, "I'm back on my own doing business consulting and enjoying it."

Maria runs her own training and consulting business. "Having my own practice allows me the freedom to 'mix and match' my skills and experience. I also have the privilege of organizing my own time and tasks. I work with Japanese companies and often answer e-mails well into the night—but then I have the time in the morning to go to water aerobics and teach private English as a second language (ESL) students!"

In an article in *Success* magazine, Lori Rosenkopf, assistant professor of management at the Wharton School, says, "You don't have to have misplaced priorities, a dysfunctional personality, and a fanatical work ethic to be a thriving entrepreneur. The creation of value through innovative products and services—the essence of entrepreneurship—can happen for any sort of person. You can be a successful entrepreneur no matter who you are."

Being self-employed can take many different forms, from buying a company or franchise to working as a contract employee or starting a consulting business. Regardless of which of these self-employment options you choose, it is crucial to your success to become very familiar with your preferences, skills, interests, and the areas that you need to develop.

Step 1: Complete the "Yearning to Be on Your Own" Self-Assessment

It is important for you to be clear about your reasons for wanting to be on your own. By revisiting your self-assessment results, you can confirm your strengths, weaknesses, needs, and desires in relation to being on your own.

Review the values you wrote down on page 31. Which ones do you think you can fulfill by being self-employed? Which of these values might not be as easily fulfilled by being on your own?

CHANGE READINESS

How did you score on the change readiness quiz on pages 39–40? As an entrepreneur, you will be dealing constantly with change in your business—with your customers and clients, in the marketplace and with the economy.

If your score indicated that you have a high level of discomfort with change, think about some ways that you can become more comfortable with change. One suggestion is to start making small changes in your routine starting today. How can you begin to be more comfortable with change?

_____

_____

_____

_____

INTERESTS

Turning an interest into a business is very common. Review the ten interests you listed in the self-assessment you took earlier on page 48. How could you incorporate one or several of these into your own business?

FAVORITE SKILLS

One reason you may want to be on your own is because you may have tired of doing work or undertaking projects that aren't interesting to you anymore. While many entrepreneurs will tell you that you will become the "chief cook and bottle washer" as a small business owner, you gain a higher level of satisfaction even by doing tedious tasks, because it's your business. Nevertheless, it's important to understand which of your favorite skills you prefer using so that you can plan your entrepreneurial situation more effectively. Review the top-ten favorite skills you listed in the self-assessment on page 56. Which of these do you want to spend the majority of your time being involved with? Write them down below:

_____

_____

_____

_____

_____

Having a strong desire to be in your own business is very important. In addition, studies of successful entrepreneurs reveal common characteristics—motivations, attitudes, personality traits, values, and beliefs. How well suited are you to being an entrepreneur? Take this brief quiz to begin to find out.

HOW DO YOU KNOW SELF-EMPLOYMENT IS FOR YOU?

1. Security isn't a very high need of mine.
   Agree   Disagree

2. I become easily bored with many things I undertake.
   Agree   Disagree

3. I am willing to commit my savings to starting my own business.
   Agree   Disagree

4. I am willing to borrow money from others, if need be.
   Agree   Disagree

5. I am very tired of a daily routine and really would like more variety.

Agree   Disagree

6. I am willing to work as long and as hard as it takes to launch my business.

Agree   Disagree

7. The idea of selling doesn't scare me.

Agree   Disagree

8. I truly see the value of networking and am willing to do it constantly.

Agree   Disagree

9. As a child or younger person, I started one or several entrepreneurial ventures.

Agree   Disagree

10. I enjoy spending time alone.

Agree   Disagree

11. I prefer solo or one-on-one activities to group activities.

Agree   Disagree

12. My work history shows a consistent pattern of stretching myself by plunging into new situations and learning new skills.

Agree   Disagree

13. Although realistic, I'm an optimistic person.

Agree   Disagree

14. My spouse or significant other and family are supportive of me.

Agree   Disagree

15. I am a decisive person who is willing to make quick decisions, even when I don't have all the information.

Agree   Disagree

16. I'm usually pretty good about asking other people for help or mentoring when I'm unsure or lack knowledge about something.

Agree   Disagree

17. Others describe me as a focused person.

Agree   Disagree

18. I am able to motivate myself consistently and maintain a high level of motivation even when under stress.

Agree   Disagree

19. I have the emotional ability to bounce back pretty quickly after setbacks or failure.

Agree   Disagree

20. When I face problems or challenges, I feel inspired to solve them.

Agree   Disagree

SCORE

Now add up the number of Agrees you circled.

15 to 20: You have the mind-set of an entrepreneur and should be able to achieve wonderful success in your own venture. Though your entrepreneurial instincts are good, be sure to write a solid business plan.

10 to 14: If you are very thorough about writing a business plan, securing financing, and getting support from your family and network, you have a very good chance for success in your own business.

9 to 13: While you have some definite learning to undergo about being self-employed, with focused passion and some education you can be successful. Perhaps you should find a partner or work as a contract employee for additional support first.

5 to 8:   Your skills and attitudes are not indicative of entre-
            preneurial success. If you are yearning to be on your
            own, you should seriously consider taking some
            classes, finding a mentor who is self-employed, and
            examining your attitudes before taking the plunge.

1 to 4:   Your score indicates that your talents may not lie in
            the entrepreneurial arena. Take another look at what
            you feel is missing in your work and think of a dif-
            ferent approach—besides starting a business—to
            fulfill your needs.

Regardless of whether your score is 20 or 1, if you undertake
a business on your own, you will experience many challenges
and obstacles along with the joy and rewards. Making a career
shift to entrepreneurism is riskier than staying in the corporate
world, so be sure to question your own motives carefully.

While many people think that having their own business automatically enables them to earn more money than they ever
have before, this may not turn out to be true. While the need to
feed and clothe yourself and your family may be very real, a truly
successful entrepreneur always has a higher purpose than earning money. You may have decided that starting your own business, rather than working as an employee for someone else, is the
only way to fulfill your need for meaning. In fact, 90 percent of
the people interviewed for this book who yearned to be self-
employed ranked the need to find meaning as having more importance than the desire to earn a lot of money. These individuals
realized that they could find their version of meaning more easily through their own business than through someone else's.

Step 2: Exploring Roadblocks and Opportunities

So you've made the decision to strike out on your own. What
next? The good news is that there are a number of options to
pursue under the umbrella of entrepreneurial ventures:

• You can opt to work as a temporary or interim employee, either in a long-term contract with one company or a series of short stints for many different organizations. In the year 2000, 28 percent of workers were "independent," and it is forecast that by 2010, 41 percent of the workforce will be employed on a contract basis.

• You can "hang out your shingle" as a solo practitioner and sell a product or provide a service. The term "soloist" became popular in the late 1990s to describe a businessperson who is more involved with doing the actual work than in building, growing, and eventually selling a business. Consultants also belong to this group. George Gendron, former editor in chief of *Inc.* magazine, calls this type of individual "a knowledge worker."

• You may decide to join the thousands of entrepreneurs who have purchased franchises. While the concept of a franchise can be appealing because of the brand that is already in place for you and the promise of training and support, there are other factors to consider, such as the up-front investment of capital, the lack of complete control over how you run your business, stiff competition, and the lifestyle of a franchise owner. These are areas you will need to research and think about carefully.

• Buying an established business that is healthy, or one that needs turning around, is yet another route to take. There are plenty of businesses for sale. Buying a business is sometimes referred to as "secondhand" entrepreneurship because the start-up phase is eliminated. *Success* magazine estimated that the annual market for small businesses in 1997 was $200 billion and growing at a rapid pace.

• Finding one or more partners and creating a limited partnership or incorporating your business is another choice. If either of these options appeals to you, you are probably serious about building a company.

How do you decide which option is right for you? Below are some pros and cons of each of the five types of entrepreneurial ventures described above, some assessments to help you determine which route is best for you, as well as some steps you will need to take toward achieving each venture.

Working as a "Free Agent"

As a temporary worker, your focus is on identifying a company that needs your specific set of skills, which enables you to negotiate your compensation as well as how and when you will deliver the work. Your mutual goal is to produce immediate results for the company. The pluses? If you want a flexible schedule, need to beef up your résumé, or are interested in trying out a certain type of work before pursuing it as a full-time employee, then becoming a free agent could be the right career move for you.

Ann is a human resources professional. At sixty-two, she has found it increasingly difficult to find full-time employment. During the boom economy of the late twentieth and early twenty-first centuries, Ann held a series of contract recruiting positions with various *Fortune* 500 companies and is thrilled that she can include these blue-chip companies on her résumé. Ann possesses a very marketable skill and as a result she has had very little "bench time."

Yet, as Ann learned, this type of work has its downside. As a contract worker, you won't usually have benefits such as health insurance and paid vacation time, nor will you have the affiliation and status you had as a full-time employee. Any company that hires you as a contractor will expect you to possess state-of-the-art skills in your field, skills that you must acquire on your own time from training that you pay for out of your own pocket. Once your current assignment has ended, you face the challenge of marketing yourself to new prospective employers. Since Ann has had health insurance benefits with only one of the companies she's worked for as a contract recruiter, she worries, at her age, about not having ongoing health coverage. And she is particularly vulnerable to the swings in the economy; as the dot.com companies started failing and employee layoffs at large corporations began to increase in 2000 and 2001, Ann found it more and more difficult to find contract recruiting positions.

Wally is an accountant who, feeling Bored and Plateaued, finally decided to leave his employer of several years when the company was taken over by new management. Wally made sure that his separation arrangement with his employer included a severance package. Because he was unsure of what he wanted to do next, Wally decided to temp, and immediately found an accounting assignment. No sooner did he start his new assignment than he realized the work bored him. Wally fulfilled his time commitment and then began another six-month assignment for a start-up company. This time, he's enjoying himself and feels challenged for the first time in years. In fact, Wally is having so much fun that he hasn't really decided whether or not he'll continue working as a free agent. Even if he decides to go to work for a company full-time after this assignment ends, Wally will approach the job market with a renewed sense of enthusiasm for his work.

Working as a Solo Practitioner

If you decide to start a business on your own without the structure of a franchise or the support of a partner, you have the advantage of being able to change gears whenever necessary to meet marketplace needs. On the other hand, you'll need to present the professional image of a company despite the fact that you *are* the company.

When you become an independent practitioner, your greatest challenge initially is to decide on, and commit to, what it is you will provide to customers or clients, whether it be a product, a service, or both. While it may be very clear to you that, for example, as a C.P.A. you will provide accounting services, you still need to ask yourself a number of questions. Do you want to specialize in serving individuals or small businesses? If you want to focus on small businesses, do you want to help small businesses in service industries only? What kinds of service industries? Where will you concentrate geographically? Is there a specific type of accounting work that you won't do, because you dislike it? Conversely, do you love working in a specific niche of accounting, and think you'd like to specialize in this?

Answering the following questions carefully will help you to narrow your business focus.

1. Do you have specific technical skills and motivated abilities that you would enjoy using in your own business? What are they? Who needs these?

   _____

   _____

   _____

   _____

2. Is there a glaring need in the marketplace that is either unfilled or burgeoning? If so, what is it?

   _____

   _____

   _____

   _____

3. Does a current trend exist in the marketplace that has created a need for, or different approach to, an established product or service? What about an anticipated trend?

   _____

   _____

_____

_____

4. Is there a very specific niche that you can fill, either because of your unique skills or a market need? What is it?

_____

_____

_____

_____

5. Is there an existing product or service that you know could be improved? Describe it.

_____

_____

_____

_____

6. Is there an established service or product that can be introduced in a different market? What is it?

_____

_____

_____

_____

7. Have you observed recurring buying patterns of individuals or corporations that can create a business opportunity for you? What are they?

_____

_____

_____

_____

8. Is there a business in another country that you could expand globally?

_____

_____

_____

_____

Answering these questions requires some serious thought and market research. It is impossible to really know what the marketplace needs without some investigation to verify your instincts about the needs that exist in your specific area of interest.

Conducting market research is a fancy way to describe the process of finding out what individuals and companies need and are willing to pay for. As a beginning entrepreneur you need to find out very quickly if you have developed a viable business idea, because even if you are in love with your idea, if very few people need it or are willing to pay for it, you will not succeed. This does not mean that you should spend an exorbitant amount of money polling thousands of people. Instead, here are some easy-to-implement ideas for discovering what the market needs and wants:

• Once you've focused in on who your target clients might be, ask potential clients the same questions (to create uniformity) one-on-one, in person, or by phone; send surveys via fax, e-mail, or by "snail" mail. Offer respondents some kind of simple and inexpensive incentive, such as a dollar bill or a book. Encourage anonymity and candid reactions.

• Run several small brainstorming sessions, facilitated by someone other than you, to generate new business ideas.

• Run several trade shows and professional association meetings where clients and other vendors or business owners meet.

• Read trade publications for market data and trends.

The type of business you operate and the clients you serve now very likely won't be the same in a year or two. Your business will evolve over time to meet marketplace trends and your own preferences and personal needs. Joy's business is a good example. When she started her own business in her early thirties, she was recruiting entry-level salespeople for commodity businesses like copier and telephone systems companies, and doing some sales training. Her recruiting activity guaranteed her income because she was able to bring some of her business from the contingency agency firm she had worked for as an employee for many years to her own business. Over time, Joy began to slow down the recruiting aspect of her business, eventually stopped recruiting altogether, and completely transitioned into sales training for the publishing industry. More recently, she has made the decision to gradually shift away from training toward giving keynote speeches.

As a solo practitioner, it isn't necessary to look like a large company by calling yourself president, or renting an office at a posh address. What is important is presenting a professional and credible image to your clients. How?

• Use a uniform approach with your marketing materials, including your business card, brochure, bio, and Web site.

• Don't print an expensive brochure initially because the services or products you provide can and will change quickly. So will the clients you work with.

• Use a professional graphic artist to design your logo. A logo is especially important if you use your name as your company name.

• Prepare a statement that succinctly describes your business to clients and anyone who asks you what you do. Your statement should briefly explain what you do and effectively describe the benefits you provide to clients: "I consult to small and medium-sized businesses helping them analyze their utility costs. I then recommend ways to reduce these costs. I guarantee a minimum cost reduction of 10 percent for any client I work with, regardless of their situation or type of business."

• Learn every aspect of running your solo practice well, before hiring someone else to do it. This includes bookkeeping, Web site management, proposal writing, and marketing. When you are confident that you can handle these areas, outsource whatever you can afford so that you can focus on developing business and delivering your service or product.

• Read Alan Weiss's book *Million Dollar Consulting*. It is an excellent guide for setting fees and analyzing the profitability of your services.

• Find three to five solo practitioners to share ideas and commiserate with about your businesses.

As a solo practitioner, you will continually experiment with how you handle different aspects of your business. Your goal should be to figure out which services or products reap the most satisfaction and profitability for you. Your limitation as a one-person business is that you have a finite amount of time to work, so be smart about managing your time by continually assessing how you spend it.

Purchasing a Franchise

A *franchise* can be described as an ongoing relationship between a *franchisor* (the granter of the franchise) and a *franchisee* (the person who is granted the franchise), which involves rights to products and services, a trademark identity, and business concepts, including a marketing and distribution system. In other words, as a franchisee, you are investing your assets in a brand and a system.

What's the upside? A franchise can provide you with quicker start-up success, a faster way to access capital to expand your business, increased earnings and marketing strength.

The cons? You have to invest a significant amount of capital up front and your control of what you consider *your* business is restricted by the franchisor. Innovation isn't always possible within the structure of the franchisor's system. You also may discover that the business doesn't truly match your lifestyle or skills.

Bill Anderson owns three Mailboxes Etc. (MBE) stores in Philadelphia and southern New Jersey. Of 3,500 MBE franchises in the United States, his stores rank in the top fifty in sales. Bill is the MBE franchise representative to the franchise advisory council of the International Franchise Organization and sits on the national board as secretary. When Bill started exploring the possibility of owning his own business, he didn't plan to be a franchisee. Instead, he saw a need for a place where the average consumer could go to make copies, send packages, and pick up mail, as an alternative to the post office. He himself had used Mailboxes Etc. and loved the concept. When he decided to start this type of business after researching his entrepreneurial options, Bill concluded that owning a franchise seemed to offer the most promising opportunity.

Bill's advice to anyone thinking about buying a franchise is to "buy a business, not a job." In other words, as he puts it, "if you are looking for a place to go every day where your definition of marketing is locking and unlocking the door," you'll never be successful as a franchisee.

Bill is adamant about the importance of believing in the specific product or service that a franchise offers customers rather than simply buying a franchise because you can afford it. Buying a quick oil change franchise when you know nothing about cars and hate to get your hands dirty is not a recipe for success.

Neither is buying a sandwich franchise when you don't enjoy dealing with food or the public.

When Bill decided that Mailboxes Etc. was the way to go, he immediately began to develop a relationship with the local Mailboxes Etc. storeowner in his hometown. Bill took him to lunch and gradually, as the owner began to trust Bill, he shared important financial information with him. The owner showed Bill his monthly royalty report, and Bill analyzed the financials, including the reveue stream, the average fixed and variable expenses, and the payroll costs.

Once Bill felt comfortable that he could satisfy his income needs as a Mailboxes Etc. franchise owner, he purchased the closest available store to his home. Today, Bill owns three stores and is successful and happy.

If you are seriously considering becoming a franchisee, you should be able to answer the following questions:

1. Do you have the kind of personality that can accept running your business according to someone else's plan without feeling that it will compromise your individuality?
2. Does each of the franchises you are looking at have a readily identifiable brand name and goodwill associated with it?
3. Will the franchise you are considering be an enjoyable place to own, manage, and work day-to-day, possibly for years?
4. Are you prepared to spend the time doing research by calling as many franchises as you can (at least ten) and visiting as many operating units as possible?
5. Would you feel proud of the product or service you are selling?
6. Is the product or service recession-proof?
7. Is the franchisor strategically minded rather than just focused on market presence? Can he or she clearly communicate this strategy to you?
8. Have you researched the competition in your area and do you feel comfortable with the potential market?

9. Do you understand the extent of operations assistance that is available?
10. Have you found a reputable lawyer who has experience with franchise agreements?

Buying a Business

According to *www.bizbuysell.com*, there are usually about two hundred to three hundred businesses for sale in the under-$1-million category per million population of any given area. This means that the opportunities for you to buy a business are many and varied. The challenge, of course, is finding the right one for you.

Glen Cooper is a certified business appraiser and past president of the Maine Business Brokers' Network in Portland, Maine. He explains the key reasons to buy an existing business:

1. You will inherit an established client base.
2. You may be able to retain experienced and loyal employees.
3. More favorable financing terms are available to you as the buyer of an established business, which can include seller financing, bank financing, and even financing by vendors.
4. An existing business has an accepted product or service, which defines its market position.
5. Established sales and marketing, accounting, inventory tracking, payroll and production systems are all in place.

If you have done your homework on the company you are thinking of buying and all of these things are truly in place, you will certainly jump-start your chances for success.

There are some downsides to buying an existing business, however.

1. The process of researching a business is tedious and taxing, especially if you aren't highly analytical or don't feel adept with financial data.

2. Finding the right business that will complement your professional experience, skills, and resources can be challenging. If you've spent your entire career in a service industry, for example, it may not make sense to consider buying a manufacturing company, because of the steep learning curve involved.

3. Even with the assistance of experts such as lawyers, accountants, insurance agents, and bankers (all of which you should take advantage of), it isn't always easy to uncover any serious problems in the company you are considering buying. Some examples of common problems that are difficult to expose: inflated income, substantial debt, or assets that have been pledged as collateral.

4. A seller often inflates the value of equipment. Always hire an independent appraiser to assess the value of equipment. If the seller of a business tells you that another buyer is about to make an offer, don't let this rush you or distract you from making a careful decision.

5. Accounts receivable problems are a common issue for most small businesses at various times. Asking to review invoices going back at least six months to identify late payers will help you understand cash-flow history or credit problems.

Below are some questions that can help you to decide whether buying a business is the right choice for you, and what you should consider in the search process.

1. What has your professional experience included (retail, manufacturing, service, finance, high tech, etc.)?

_____

_____

_____

_____

2. How long do you want to spend searching for the right business to buy? How many hours a day or week are you willing to commit?

_____

_____

_____

_____

3. Are you willing to move or commute a long distance if necessary?

_____

_____

_____

_____

4. How involved with the management of your business do you want to be? Do you see your role as an investor only, as the person who hires the people who will run it day-to-day, or as the one who will step in as the hands-on leader?

_____

_____

_____

_____

5. Do you have a strong network of advisers, vendors or suppliers, and potential clients in certain industries? Who are they?

_____

_____

_____

_____

6. How large do you want your business to be?

_____

_____

_____

_____

7. Do you want a business that has had steady growth with a stable cash flow or one that has more growth potential and not as consistent a cash flow?

_____

_____

_____

_____

8. Are you interested in buying a company that needs to be turned around?

_____

_____

_____

_____

9. How much cash do you have available, including potential assets, profit sharing, stocks and bonds, and savings that you can liquidate to invest in a business?

_____

_____

_____

_____

10. Do you have contacts with bankers, venture capitalists, or angel investors? Who are they?

_____

_____

_____

_____

11. How soon do you need to see profits?

_____

_____

_____

_____

While these are some guidelines to contemplate, be careful not to narrow your search too much. There are many complementary industries that you may not have thought about. For example, if you're a sports enthusiast, instead of looking only at sporting goods stores, why not consider buying a small magazine or Web site that specializes in sports?

If you don't know where you can find businesses that are for sale, here are some suggestions:

- Listen to word-of-mouth from your professional network, friends, and acquaintances.
- Seek out trusted advisers such as your attorney, accountant, banker, doctor, or dentist.
- Trade associations can be very helpful if you've narrowed your search down to the type of industry you're interested in. They all have local meetings and many have newsletters or Web sites.
- Cold-calling owners of businesses can uncover businesses for sale that haven't yet been advertised or listed with a broker. You can find the names of companies in the yellow pages, from local chamber of commerce membership lists, or simply by driving through commercial areas and writing down names.
- Read newspaper and trade publication classified advertisements.
- Search the Internet by industry or business broker. Or look at the Web sites of businesses in which you are interested.
- Use a business broker, but remember that brokers nearly always represent the seller of a business, not the buyer. A successful business broker will offer you a large selection of listings or specialize in the area you've targeted.

Remember: If the owner of a company has never sold a business before, he or she can tend to overvalue the business *and* be emotional in the process. Doing your homework thoroughly costs money and takes time, but is well worth it in the long run. If you are organized in your approach, however, you may become the proud owner of an established and profitable business. Remember the number of small businesses cited at the beginning of this chapter? Eight million businesses—and all you need is one!

Creating a Partnership

Finding the right person to partner with in your own business is analogous to getting married. To be successful, you want to have the same values, be compatible day-to-day, accept each other's limitations while leveraging strengths. Most important, you must trust each other.

You may already have a business idea and have decided to find a partner, or you may be talking to someone about first becoming business partners, and then identifying the type of business you'd like to start. Either way, you should be extremely cautious about the person you will probably spend more time with than your spouse. Some suggestions for assessing your prospective business partner are:

- Collaborate with him or her on a project or a cross-selling effort before committing to a full-time partnership. Doing this will give you the chance to observe the other person's working style and see how he or she handles business overall.
- Have a serious discussion about each other's vision for your business. Are they in sync or worlds apart?
- Be careful about partnering with someone who is too similar to you. Be sure your prospective business partner has strengths and expertise that you don't possess, and vice versa.
- Be very sure that your partner will take the financial and legal responsibilities of starting a business seriously.
- Have a discussion about who will be in charge of each area of the company.
- Once you've decided to proceed with your partnership, write down your expectations of each other about responsibilities and tasks.
- Hire a lawyer to draft a partnership agreement for you, of which the most important component is a mechanism for ending your partnership.
- Investigate the legal and tax implications of a general partnership, a corporation, or a limited liability corporation before deciding on which to use for your business.

A business partnership requires constant communication and hard work; however, it can be very rewarding to have a partner who shares your dream of running a successful business.

Roadblocks and Obstacles

There are obstacles that all potential entrepreneurs encounter, regardless of which route they take. You can address these roadblocks, however, so that you can deal with them ahead of time.

Selling. Whether you like it or not, when you are an entrepreneur, *you are always selling.* Your perseverance at sales and your ability to sell will be one of the most critical factors in your success. "Attitudes and Behaviors That Create Small Business Success," a survey conducted by Yankelovich, found that a dominant concern of the more than two thousand entrepreneurs questioned was attracting and keeping clients, outranking worries about staffing, paying the bills, and competition.

Unfortunately, unless you have worked in sales, or have been responsible for revenue as a sales manager, the whole area of sales may be very foreign to you. Whether you lack experience, have a dislike for the act of selling, or don't think it's how you should be spending your time, it is important that you overcome your specific emotional and practical obstacles and embrace the idea that as an entrepreneur, you are a professional salesperson.

If necessary, you can hire a sales coach who specializes in working with small business owners, or take classes or workshops offered by private companies and colleges and universities. Hundreds of books have been written on the subject, many of which are geared toward the person who has never sold anything before.

If you are sure that you want to go into your own business, you should begin your education in sales. Waiting until the day you open your doors doesn't make good sense. The best way to become a good salesperson is to sell, and keep selling. Start now by selling your business idea to others.

If you have both a marketing plan and sales goals (the basic components of a business plan; see step 4 on page 173) and feel passionate about your business, selling will not be as difficult as you think. Sales techniques are learned like any other technical ability and success is a matter of using specific skills, rather than a reflection of how dynamic, extroverted, and bright you are. One of the greatest challenges an entrepreneur faces is maintaining sales activity while fulfilling orders or delivering service. If you've ever taken a "Sales 101" course, you know that the pipeline of prospective clients must constantly be fed. Doing this successfully requires focus and discipline, above all.

Cash flow. One of the biggest worries that nearly everyone has about starting their own business is giving up a steady salary and being anxious about not being able to pay their bills, both personally and professionally. This is a valid concern. In a perfect world, having twelve to eighteen months' worth of cash put away in anticipation of the ups and downs of a new business (or any business, for that matter) should solve the problem. But the truth is that most people don't have the ability to save that much money and end up starting their business with a smaller financial cushion. So what's the answer? If delaying starting your business for six or eight months means you'll be able to save more money, then this is a wise strategy. If your fear about not having enough money is paralyzing you from moving forward, however, then set a goal for starting your business within a specific time frame and don't let yourself off the hook.

Most people who start a business do so with savings, credit card cash advances, loans from friends and family, and severance payments. The reality is that you will only be able to invest whatever it is you have at your disposal, as well as the amount of money that is comfortable for you.

Elizabeth started her business with money from a 401(k) plan from her last employer. This provided her with the ability to pay all of her expenses for four months. Most financial planners or accountants would not recommend this as a strategy, but it was Elizabeth's only viable option at the time. Did it create stress for her knowing that she was operating in a four-month window? Absolutely! Yet, Elizabeth also knew that she could borrow money from several friends if the need arose. Her fear motivated her to hustle and drum up business quickly, which she did. She had gone through the process of budgeting every single expense and was more aware of how much it cost for her to live and work than ever before in her life.

Some procedures you can put in place to help your cash flow stream once you're in business are:

- Offer a small discount for early or on-time payment. Most accounts payable departments are trained to treat early-payment invoices as a priority.
- Request a deposit for project work or a large contract. Be sure to have your client sign a contract stating the exact terms of their payment for your products or services.
- Ask for a monthly retainer for ongoing work. This also delivers the message to your client that you value your relationship and assures your availability.
- Arrange follow-up services or products as part of the overall package you sell to your client. Obviously, in addition to helping your cash flow, you are creating residual revenue.
- Be sure you are charging fair market fees and prices. Just because you are new in your business does not mean that you should undercut your prices. Ask your competition about their pricing and ask your clients what they pay your competition.
- Have a set of goals and a strategy in place for collecting cash, including a plan for seriously delinquent payments. Don't be afraid to use outside assistance if you need to.

Lack of a support system, resources, and feedback. As an entrepreneur, it can be very lonely not to have people and resources surrounding you when you need them the most. Even if you are running a company with employees, they won't necessarily be able to provide you with the support you'll need. This means that you should immediately find or create external opportunities to supply you with this often-unfulfilled need.

Networking is necessary to your success as an entrepreneur for generating sales leads. It is also a wonderful vehicle for finding other people who are in situations like your own to compare notes with and learn from. There are many structured networking groups and associations both local and national in scope. Find out what they are by asking everyone you know which groups they belong to and which ones they find most valuable. Don't just network when business is slow or when you're feeling guilty about not doing it. Make it part of your weekly schedule.

Creating a small advisory board of people who are at various levels of experience in running their own businesses is a fabulous way to learn and share your experiences. You can schedule formal meetings or communicate more informally on an as-needed basis.

Hiring a business coach who specializes in working with start-up business owners or established business owners will provide ongoing support that you will take seriously because you are paying for it.

Involve your family in your business. You will be working much harder than you ever did before and, whether you like it or not, this will eat into your family and personal time. Asking your family for advice or a different perspective helps them feel included in your business, and often they will surprise you with some great ideas.

Blending your work and your life. There is no question that if you want to be successful in your own business, you will work harder and longer than you ever did as an employee. The time you spend with work and leisure will blur, partially because of technology that enables you to work twenty-four hours a day, and also because you can always be doing something else to take care of your business. Even if you have an attorney, an accountant, a payroll service, an assistant, and a bookkeeper, you are now wearing every single functional hat in your company. If you're not planning, you are selling; if you're not updating your Web site, you're solving a problem—and on and on.

Before you start your business, write down how much time (in hours) you spend a week or month involved with the categories below. If you're not sure, then track a typical week to find out. Next to that number, write down how much time you would like to spend doing those things when you start your own business.

Work _____
Commuting to work _____
Outside interests/hobbies/sports _____
Exercise _____
Vacation _____
Family and relatives _____
Religious and spiritual activities _____
Volunteer work _____
Personal business _____
Other (add your own) _____

Refer to this list every three months to see if you have been able to maintain the balance you'd like to have in your life as a new entrepreneur. Getting a new business up and running is, at least initially, a twenty-four-hour proposition, and finding "true" balance may not be possible for a while.

Step 3: Create an Action Plan

A Vision Statement for Your Business

It is extremely important to remember that success is, as the cliché goes, "in the eye of the beholder." Most likely, your vision of success varies greatly from your neighbor's vision. What is important is that before you start your own business, you are able to articulate your vision—to yourself and to your family. In just a moment, you'll learn how to write a business plan where you'll include many of your specific measurable goals. While your revenue and income and the number of clients you serve are certainly important, they are only a part of how you'll define and measure your success. Developing a brief written vision statement for your business is a good way to capture your business concept. This vision is what you would like your business to become; it often includes your unique selling proposition, more commonly known as a USP. Your USP is that characteristic or feature of the business that differentiates you from your competition.

An example of a vision statement: To be recognized nationally as a leader in presentation skills services, providing innovative training, coaching, facilitating, and consulting services to our clients.

What is your vision statement?

_____

_____

_____

_____

_____

Writing a Business Plan

Regardless of what type of business you are starting, writing a business plan is very important. This is a required document if you are seeking external financial assistance, whether you are approaching a bank, private investor, or a venture capitalist. Even if you're relying solely on your personal assets to finance your business, the process that you go through to write your plan is as valuable as the outcome itself. A business plan is a road map for your success as an entrepreneur. There is software available for you to use as a template for your business plan, as well as innumerable books you can read on the subject. The basic components of every plan are: a company overview, executive summary, marketing plan, management plan, and financial plan.

COMPANY OVERVIEW—The company overview includes both short- and long-term projections of sales, profits, market penetration, and any other measures of progress of the success of your business. The type of business you are becoming involved with (buying a business, buying a franchise, or starting a business from scratch) and the way you plan on structuring the company are also part of the company overview. With the advice of a lawyer and an accountant, you may want to become a limited liability corporation (LLC or sole proprietorship), a partnership, or an "S" or "C" corporation. The way you structure your company is important for liability and tax issues. Pages 250–51 in the Resources guide lists books that will give you guidance in this area.

Additionally, you should list the type of taxes you'll pay as a business and as an employer, as well as all legal requirements such as licensing and local, state, and federal regulations and laws. The last two items you'll include in the overview are the kinds and amount of insurance protection you'll need along with the types of advisers with whom you plan to consult.

EXECUTIVE SUMMARY—This is a brief (no more than three pages) opening description written to grab the reader's attention. It's a snapshot of your company, including the market opportunity you are pursuing, your product or service, facts and figures about your target clients, a competitive strategy, your management team (if relevant), and a financial summary. Since this is the most difficult and the most important part of your business plan to write, you should write it last.

THE MARKETING PLAN—The best way to describe the marketing plan is that it indicates how you'll take in money. While the word "marketing" is used, this portion of your business plan is primarily focused on selling. It outlines how you propose to sell your products or services, how you plan on bringing them to the attention of prospective clients, and at what price. To write your marketing plan, ask yourself the following questions:

1. What do you propose to make or provide as a service?
2. To whom do you hope to sell it (prospective clients) and why will they buy it?
3. How many prospective clients are there and where are they?
4. What is your competition and how will you capture a share of the market?
5. What prices or fees do you plan on charging, and how did you calculate them?
6. How and where will you deliver your products or services?
7. How will you promote your new business (Internet, advertising, direct selling, networking, etc.)?
8. How will you keep your clients happy (deal with complaints, provide customer service)?

THE MANAGEMENT PLAN—While your marketing plan describes how you'll take in money, the management plan describes how you are going to spend it as well as how you will structure and operate your business. Write your management plan using the following questions as guidelines:

1. What will you name your business? Thomson & Thomson (*www.thomson-thomson.com*) and Corsearch (*www.corsearch.com*) are two companies that, for a fee, will let you do a trademark

search via their Web sites, check federal and state registrations, Internet domain names, and listings in phone books as well as trade publications. You can choose to register your name with the Patent and Trademark Office of the United States government, which will keep your company name protected anywhere in the United States and on the Internet.

2. How will you manage your business day-to-day?

3. Where will you locate your business? This may be crucial for a restaurant, for example, but not at all for a solo consultant.

4. What equipment and furniture will you need and how much will they cost?

5. What kind of phone service and office equipment will you need and how much will they cost?

6. Will you need materials or inventory and who will supply them and at what price?

7. Do you plan to hire employees? What skills and qualifications will they need? How much will you pay them?

8. What records will you keep? How will you keep track of taxes, insurance, lease information, employee payroll and benefits and so on?

9. Who will do your bookkeeping and accounting?

THE FINANCIAL PLAN—This translates your business into dollars and cents. It spells out how much you think it will cost to get started and operate for one or more years, how much you think you'll need to take in from sales, and how much you will need to borrow to make your entrepreneurial vision a reality.

You should detail your costs of operating for the first year, or until the break-even point. This should include every item that will cost your business money: rent, utilities, taxes, salaries, employee benefits, postage, marketing costs, office supplies, and so forth. Include everything! You will develop this information by preparing a budget for your start-up year and each year thereafter.

You should present how much money you expect to take in during your first year in business or until you break even, and the total amount you will need to get started and keep your business functioning.

The amount of money that you plan to invest from your own resources—savings, credit card cash advances, a severance payment, or refinancing your mortgage (home-equity loan)—and the amount you will borrow from your friends and family should be listed.

If you are planning to borrow money from your bank or another outside source, they will be interested in all of the information in your business plan and what your business experience and management capabilities are. They will also ask for a financial statement covering your personal assets, liabilities, and any collateral you are prepared to put up.

You can attach supporting documents such as résumés; references from creditors, potential clients, and suppliers; a lease agreement; relevant contracts; partnership agreements; and documentation of your company structure.

Even if you choose not to write a business plan when you're starting your business, doing so when you're thinking of expanding your business, or you're experiencing problems in your business, or you'd like to take a more strategic approach to running your business will prove to be a tremendously helpful exercise. Obviously, it is optimum to write a business plan when starting from the ground up, but not everyone does so.

Twenty-Six Things You Should Do
When Starting Your Business

As you start planning your new business, here are some of the things you should do. Do note that these suggestions are not necessarily in order or relevant to every type of entrepreneurial venture. Check off each one as you do it.

□ 1. Interview three entrepreneurs and ask them to share their best advice with you.

□ 2. Identify your business niche and write a brief mission statement explaining your niche. Also known as your "two-minute drill" or your defining statement, this is different from your company vision.

□ 3. Get two or three referrals to accountants. Meet and interview them.

□ 4. Do the same for an attorney and for a financial planner.

□ 5. Get a long-term disability policy before you quit your job.

□ 6. Investigate your health-insurance options.

□ 7. Name your business.

□ 8. Decide on your business structure now. Will your business be an LLC, a "C," or an "S" corporation?

□ 9. Get an employer identification number (EIN) for IRS purposes. Call 800-TAX-FORM or ask your accountant how to do this.

□ 10. Get licenses and permits. Depending on your business, you can contact your city's business license department, the city zoning board, or the health department.

□ 11. Set up a Web site.

□ 12. List your personal assets.

□ 13. Make a budget for your personal expenses.

□ 14. If you need financing, get it while you are still working.

□ 15. Find a location. If you are planning on working from home, check IRS requirements. If you need retail or commercial space, consider accessibility, proximity to competitors, taxes, insurance, utilities, and maintenance.

□ 16. Open a business checking account.

□ 17. Research equipment. You'll need a computer, printer, scanner, modem, DSL or cable line, copier, phone, postage meter, cell phone or pager, among other things.

□ 18. Be sure you have technical support lined up for all of your equipment.

☐ 19. Find a graphic artist to design your logo, business cards, and stationery and get them printed.

☐ 20. Find suppliers through trade shows, buyers' directories, trade publications, business-to-business yellow pages, and referrals.

☐ 21. Get merchant credit card status. American Express and Discover can be contacted directly. Visa and MasterCard accounts are established through your bank.

☐ 22. Create a credit application for customers.

☐ 23. Advertise job openings on the Internet and in local newspapers.

☐ 24. Create a job application, making sure it meets legal guidelines.

☐ 25. Get relevant business insurance, such as workers' compensation, liability, property/casualty, or automobile.

☐ 26. Start networking and generating business.

The beauty of starting your own business is that it's yours to do with what you want. As an entrepreneur, you'll have your unique fingerprint on your business. Here are two success stories to illustrate the point.

After twenty-eight years in information technology, Harry wanted more meaning and balance as well as "to live more fully." He decided to start a personal and business coaching company, which he named All About Enterprises. When asked if he was satisfied with his new business, he replied, "Very satisfied! My new business is tied to my core values (by design!). I really like the idea of more flexibility and control of my time and focus. I believe that I can build upon my fifteen years of consulting to build my own coaching/training practice."

After eleven years with Citibank, Sheri resigned from her position as a vice president and started a business, Cotton Candy Kids, which designs and creates custom children's accessories. Sheri expresses well what so many entrepreneurs feel: "Cotton Candy Kids is a perfect blend for me at this time in my life. It allows me to stay home with my children, put my creative 'juices' to work, have a sense of accomplishment, meet new people, and keep the brain working! I have always loved sewing and needed a creative outlet. Someone once told me, 'When you do what you love for a living, it's as easy as breathing.' The business has really taken off and the path has felt as natural as breathing. It rejuvenates my mind and soul."

The process of starting a business can be overwhelming, and you will find very quickly that some entrepreneurial options are a better fit for you than others. Once you've identified the one or two options you'd like to explore, do the first thing on the list of twenty-six suggestions you just read: find several people who are doing what you think you'd like to do and talk to them about their experience and recommendations they have for you to get started.

CHAPTER 10

One Toe in the Retirement Pool

In 2001, the American Association of Retired Persons (AARP), the powerful advocacy group for people older than fifty, reported that of its 34 million members, 67 percent—nearly 23 million people—said that they would continue working because they wanted to. In the dictionary, retirement is defined as "going away from business or public life" or "concluding one's working or professional life." A Gallup poll commissioned by Paine Webber, however, showed that 85 percent of retiring boomers say they plan on working after retirement.

Today, age is not necessarily an indicator that you should retire. Someone who retires at age sixty-five could have twenty or twenty-five years left to live. According to the Federal Interagency Forum on Aging, the sixty-five-and-older segment of the population will double to 70 million between 2000 and 2030. A good percentage of these people will still want to work—doing what they had done previously or becoming involved in something that will be different, but they will still work.

If you are eyeing "retirement" in the next several years, are about to retire now, or have already retired and still want to work in some way, the first step is to think long and hard about why you are considering retirement. Among your reasons may be the following:

1. You're just ready to retire. You've thought about it for a while and though you aren't necessarily sure about what you'll do when you retire, you know that it's time. You've tired of the grind of working or you have had numerous unhappy job situations and just don't want to participate on the battlefield that work can be at times.

John, at fifty-six, manages a worldwide business for a health-care company in clinical diagnostics and marketing and has worked since he was sixteen and a half. He just isn't interested in working anymore. He thinks about retirement constantly and believes that many of his peers are doing so as well.

2. Your spouse or significant other is in the same stage of life as you and is also ready to retire or has done so recently. While it isn't necessary to retire side by side with your partner, the adjustment period that goes along with not working full-time and changing your lifestyle is easier to go through with someone else. Surrounding yourself with friends, former colleagues, relatives, and peers to socialize with and count on as a support group makes retirement so much more pleasurable. If you know enough people who are in the same phase of life that you are, retiring can be even more attractive.

3. You want to retire while you're still in good health so that you can fully enjoy your retirement years. Even if you are in good physical shape now, you may experience health problems as a result of normal aging, some of which you won't be able to anticipate or control. On the other hand, if you're not as healthy as you used to be, retirement is less stressful than working full-time. As the saying goes, "If you don't have your health, you don't have anything."

4. You're reasonably comfortable with the financial aspects of

retirement. Income and finances are usually the first thing that people focus on when thinking about taking this step—not surprisingly, since these are also the topics that cause the most concern. Many people do not have a company pension plan and many others have experienced unforeseen financial reversals in their lives, such as failed investments, shifts in the stock market, or huge uninsured medical expenses. The majority of people retiring will suffer a drop in income no matter what their situation is. While John fantasizes about retiring, he knows that in order to live the lifestyle that he and his wife desire, he can't realistically retire until he's sixty-two. "Having enough to be able to live on with what we have stored away" is his serious concern. He's willing to "hang in there" for another six years in order to ensure that this will happen.

5. Family issues such as caring for your elderly parents and spending more time with your grandchildren have become more important. While the focus of this chapter is on older individuals, this category also includes those who aren't necessarily older but have found it too difficult to effectively manage both a career and a family. Keri, only thirty-four, loved her career as a vice president of recruiting for an investment bank but has decided to "retire" to spend time with her children and husband. "I found a lot of satisfaction in managing a career and love my time now with my family. I'd like to try to have both, but am not sure I can do it and feel satisfied or competent at both."

6. You have a lot of hobbies and interests you yearn to become more involved with, or you'd like to develop certain skills or expertise that you haven't taken the time to do while working.

Several, or all, of these reasons can significantly influence why, when, and how you choose to retire. Take some time to think about each one and decide its relevance to your specific situation.

Step 1: Complete the "One Toe in the Retirement Pool" Self-Assessment

Retiring from your full-time career will enable you to be flexible about the kind of work you'll do and how you'll do it, giving you the opportunity to explore interests, hobbies, or another kind of work.

Review your top-ten values on page 31 to remind yourself of what's important to you.

Next, review the interests and favorite skills you wrote down on pages 48 and 56, as they will provide the foundation for the type of work you'll find or create. Are there several interests you'd like to get involved with when you retire? Write them down below.

_____

_____

_____

_____

Now do the same for your favorite skills. List the ones that you would like to use for the first time or continue using once you've created your retired life.

_____

_____

_____

_____

Now, keeping your self-assessment results in mind, ask yourself, "If I could do any work in the world after I 'retire,' what would it be? Where would I do it? With whom would I be doing it?"

_____

_____

_____

_____

_____

Once you've refamiliarized yourself with the results of your self-assessment, it's time to do some thinking and exploring about your retirement.

Answering these simple questions can help you ascertain the additional soul-searching and research you need to do to help you plan for retirement:

1. Have you always thought you'd retire at a certain age? If so, what is it?

_____

_____

_____

2. What are or were your reasons for picking this age?

_____

_____

_____

3. Have you already met with a financial planner to plan for retirement?

_____

_____

_____

4. If not, why haven't you?

_____

_____

_____

5. Do you have an up-to-date will, a revocable trust, and appropriate insurance coverage for you and your family?

_____

_____

_____

6. How do you feel about retiring? Have you really sat down and thought through the possible positive and negative implications of it?

_____

_____

_____

7. Can you picture what retirement would look like for you from a lifestyle standpoint (where you'll live, your proximity to your family, etc.)?

_____

_____

_____

8. Have you had a serious discussion with your spouse and immediate family about retiring?

_____

_____

_____

9. If so, what are their concerns about it?

_____

_____

_____

10. If not, when do you plan on doing so?

_____

_____

_____

11. Do you know anyone who has retired within the last several years? If so, have you had an earnest conversation with them about what they've experienced so far?

_____

_____

_____

Retirement as we've known it is being transformed into a different type of transition phase. You must prepare yourself emotionally, psychologically, and financially for this new phase, whether it means you're working or not. To do so, you must talk to people, research, and be very thoughtful about who you are. You must know what your goals are in life, and what makes you happy as well as fulfilled. Nowadays, it is quite likely that you will live a very long time after you "retire."

Step 2: Exploring Roadblocks and Opportunities

Your Finances

A survey by SunAmerica revealed that 80 percent of all Americans between the ages of twenty-five and fifty-five are concerned that they won't have enough money to retire. Most of the people interviewed admitted that they had never tried to calculate how much they would need to save in order to maintain their current lifestyle in retirement.

Your retirement income will be financed by any investments you may have, Social Security, pension plans, real estate, and income you generate from working. You may not have all of these sources of income when you retire, so planning how much you will have is very important.

Phased retirement plans will become more and more prevalent as time goes on. These allow older workers to leave a company gradually over a period of five years or so. The employer distributes the worker's pension withdrawal, compensation, and medical benefits incrementally over time. Unfortunately, though, according to a 1999 study by Watson Wyatt, only 19 percent of companies in the United States offered phased retirement programs. While this number will continue to increase in the future, you won't necessarily have the advantage of this benefit.

The sad truth is that many people who retire depend almost solely on Social Security for income, despite the fact that it was never intended to provide 100 percent of a retiree's income. In fact, in 1999, Social Security provided more than half the total annual income for the majority of all Americans older than age sixty-five. According to Mike Robbins, author of the *Smart Guide to Planning for Retirement,* the Social Security program is currently designed to replace about 42 percent of the "average" retiree's preretirement income. On top of this dismal reality, Social Security has been in trouble for a long time, and the future looks bleak, unless the entire system is overhauled. According to the Social Security Administration, by 2011, when the first baby boomers hit the official retirement age of sixty-seven, the ratio of workers to retirees will be somewhere between 2.5 to 1. When the program began in 1935, this ratio was 50 workers to every 1 retiree. This is a significant statistic because the people who are working are the ones who continue to fund Social Security. Mike Robbins advises that when calculating the retirement income you'll need, you should factor in a longer than usual life span, inflation, and the fact that your money will keep working for you while you are retired.

One way to ease your financial worries for retirement is to hire a financial planner. When you are selecting a financial planner, use the following criteria:

1. Is the person as interested in your values, lifestyle, and goals as he or she is in your financial situation?
2. Is he or she approachable, empathic, and a good listener?
3. Does he or she have a definite philosophy about building wealth?
4. Is he or she willing to share his or her personal portfolio with you? In other words, does he do for himself what he advises others to do?
5. Does he or she have specific experience with individuals planning retirement? What has his track record been with these clients? Can you interview a few of them?

Whether you use a financial planner or do the numbers on your own, you may find—depending on your situation, the economy, and shifting societal attitudes—that you may need to keep working longer than you had hoped. John, the health-care executive, is a good example of this. He has another six years to retirement and believes that planning for retirement is "like a chess game. It's important to position properly all the pieces of retirement—your 401(k), your pension if you have one, your IRA, medical insurance, your investments, and all the other financial tools that are relevant to your well-being." He goes on to say, "The other important part of thinking about retiring is 'where.' Where do you want to live?"

Choosing Where to Live When You're Retired

In *Retirement on a Shoestring*, John Howells recommends places to retire, ranging from Mexico and Costa Rica to Oklahoma and Mississippi. Since his targeted readership is those people who must get by in retirement solely on Social Security, Howells is more focused on the cost of living than on other lifestyle issues, such as community services and culture.

While a lower cost of living is important to many retirees, other reasons to move to a different state are for a better climate, community services geared toward the elderly, medical care, an easier lifestyle, and a greater availability of property and land. The U.S. Census Bureau has projected that by the year 2020, Nevada, Arizona, Colorado, Utah, Washington, Georgia, Alaska, and California will double their older populations, for many of these reasons.

If you are considering moving to a different state, region, or another country, be sure to visit for a week and talk to some of the residents, including people who have moved there to retire. Some of the things you should look for when you're exploring a new geographic area to live are:

- *Climate.* While warm weather may be appealing, can you handle suffocating summers?
- *Taxes.* What are property tax, state income tax, and sales tax?
- *Housing.* Are there houses that are appealing to you? Rental communities? Continuing-care housing? Shared housing?
- *Medical care.* Is there an adequate hospital? Are there enough doctors to take care of the community? Do you have a special health problem that can be monitored and taken care of?
- *Transportation.* Are there taxis and buses, and is there easy accessibility to the closest airport?
- *Proximity to your family and friends.* Is it easy to visit you? Is it a place that people will find appealing to visit?
- *Culture.* Are there museums, a theater, a symphony? Are there libraries close by?

- *Social interactions.* Are there people in the community to whom you can relate with similar cultural backgrounds or interests?
- *Services for the elderly.* What kinds of community services exist for the aging?
- *Education.* Are there colleges or universities nearby where you can take classes?
- *Your interests.* Is this an area where you can involve yourself in your particular interest, such as art and music, fishing, hunting, skiing, tennis, or golf?
- *Industry.* What kinds of businesses exist? Are there companies where you can work full-time or part-time?
- *Safety.* Is the crime rate low? Will you feel comfortable walking or driving around the area?
- *Affordability.* How much do food, gas, utilities, movie tickets, and clothing cost? How much does it cost to eat out in a restaurant? What is the overall cost of living?

What Kind of Work Do You Want to Do in Retirement?

The Futurist magazine predicts that "increasingly, over time, people will work at one career, 'retire' for a while when they can afford it, return to school, begin another career, and so on in endless variations. True retirement, a permanent end to work, will be delayed until very late in an extended life." Indeed, you may be part of the growing trend of older workers who are staying in the workforce. In some ways, you are not unlike many of the people who fit into the other five situations in this book. Whether you are Bored and Plateaued or wondering Where's the Meaning?, the first thing you must do is to get reacquainted with yourself so that you can focus your goals and energy in the appropriate direction.

Michael did just this when he retired at age sixty-five and moved from New York City to Cape Cod, where he had owned a home for years. He started helping a local florist part-time and now works three or four days a week delivering flowers. He tells stories about the times when he rings someone's doorbell and the person opens the door to see Michael standing there with a bouquet of flowers. It gives him joy to see the delighted expression on that individual's face. He helps many elderly recipients of flowers find a vase, keeping them company for a few minutes. Michael, who worked as an executive in the out-placement business for many years, frankly never expected to get so much pleasure out of a task like delivering flowers, but he always knew that having meaning in his work was important.

Have you always wanted to start your own business? Maybe you didn't think you could afford to or weren't willing to make the sacrifices when you were in your peak working years. Lee was reorganized out of a twenty-five-year career and, at fifty-seven, as he's eyeing retirement, he is on his own as a broker of award products for the incentive industry. He loves the independence and plans on dabbling in this business even when he slows down his work schedule.

Ernie enjoyed a very satisfying career as a product sales manager for a large chemical company. Over sixty, he officially retired from his job and immediately began pursuing opportunities to become a speaker with an emphasis on selling. In the beginning stages of his exploration of the speaking business, Ernie hired a coach to help him create a one-hour speech, and began learning more about the craft of speaking by joining Toastmasters (a national association that focuses on teaching people to speak) and several speakers' associations. He also started networking with his contacts in the chemical business to learn about possible speaking opportunities. While Ernie is excited about this new part-time "career," he also is very adamant about the fact that his "basic thrust is to work at a level that will keep me interested and challenged, with the money being a secondary consideration."

What about simply working to fulfill some of your social needs, your need to be useful, or to supplement your income? In a June 2000 *Parade* magazine article, "Retire from Life? Never!," Neal Cole, eighty, tells a story of his work at Portland International Airport in Oregon doing security check-ins and pushing wheelchairs for travelers in need. He makes $6.50 an hour and another $15 or $20 a day in tips. As he says, "I get to talk to a lot of people and I've lost forty pounds."

Zetta is eighty-three and works at the "Top of the Falls" souvenir shop in Niagara Falls, New York, during the peak tourist season, from April to October. She had never had a steady career, opting instead to raise her three children full-time. On occasion, she had worked as a jewelry engraver, an independent salesperson, a bank teller, and a clerical assistant. After not working for thirty years, Zetta took a job in the gift shop and has worked there for fourteen years. She explains that while she never gets bored while home alone, she does get lonely, and enjoys her interaction with the tourists. Zetta admits that if she didn't have to show up for work, she wouldn't stay active. The best part? "I love meeting people. Sometimes I make an instant connection with someone, and even if I know I may never see the person again, I feel as if I have a friend for life." Zetta teaches herself German, using audiotapes and videotapes, and has fun trying to talk to the many German-speaking tourists who visit Niagara Falls. She makes only $7.00 an hour, which supplements her Social Security. While the small amount of money helps, the other benefits far outweigh the financial ones.

Corporations are learning that retaining, retraining, and hiring older workers is a smart business strategy. In an era in which the ability to find workers with the right skills has become more difficult for companies, the older worker is often the solution to this problem. A January 2001 article in the Money and Business section of the *New York Times,* "To Be Old, Gifted and Employed Is No Longer Rare," profiled several octogenarians and nonagenarians who still work full-time in very professional roles. The article explained, "The number of very, very old workers is growing largely because of the blazing demand for labor in recent years and the stunning growth in the number of older people. When the United States was born, one of every 40 people was over 65. Today, one in seven is, and by 2030 one in four will be, the Census Bureau has predicted. Older people today are also healthier, on average, making it easier for them to keep working."

In addition to the marketplace's need for talented labor and a greater availability of people in older age groups, there are other reasons that make it sensible to hire older workers:

• Bringing back people who had worked at a corporation previously helps to preserve the corporate memory, a crucial component of a corporate culture.

• Rapid changes in the job market and technology have necessitated the need for additional education and retraining for every level of employee. More and more, even small companies see this as a necessary investment rather than an expense. Also, the traditional bias toward training only new employees or senior managers appears to be diminishing. This creates a willingness to hire the older worker and to train him or her alongside everyone else.

• The *New York Times* article cited the results of a Harris poll, which asked 774 corporate human resources directors about older workers. Of those interviewed, 80 percent agreed that older workers (age fifty-five and up) had less turnover, and 71 percent said these workers had as much ability as younger employees to acquire new skills. Yet, according to AARP data, while work ethic, loyalty, and experience rank high on employer surveys about the traits possessed by older workers, inflexibility and a lack of technical skills are cited as being the downside to these employees.

Melanie has had a successful career as an insurance under-writer and loved the technical aspects of her work, and, like many of us, Melanie has suffered through many less-than-enjoyable work situations. A year or so after her husband retired, Melanie found herself in yet another difficult and stressful work environment and decided to retire to keep her husband company as well as to restore her psychological well-being. She stopped working, traveled, read, and caught up on projects she hadn't been able to do while working. The first year or so was great, but Melanie, only in her early fifties, began to feel antsy. While she did retire at an earlier age than most people do, she feels that if she had put more time into planning her retirement, she would have experienced more satisfaction. She went back to work, but in a job that was at a much lower level than any of her previous positions, and while the challenge and the status no longer existed, the long hours and demands on her were still there. On top of this, her compensation was much reduced from when she worked as an underwriter. She eventually left that job, and at fifty-five, took a job comparable to the one she had left before she retired. She plans on retiring again at fifty-nine and a half, but this time she says her approach will be different. She will spend more time preparing herself mentally, and planning her affairs before she actually retires. Her advice? "Take the time to plan your retirement. It should be approached just like a job search. If you don't, you may be shocked by what you'll experience when you retire."

Step 3: Create an Action Plan

It's nice to know that as you are approaching retirement, you have a wide array of options available to you. Whether you are "chomping at the bit" to retire and never work again (15 percent of people planning retirement don't want to work at all) or excited about starting a second part-time career, there are some things you should think about and do before you take the plunge. Examine the details of your life as if you are doing "due diligence" to buy a business:

• All of the many financial details that are so important to your retirement should be scrutinized and analyzed by you and by experts. As Mike Robbins says in his book, *Smart Guide to Planning for Retirement,* "Retirement is the single largest financial goal most of us face."

• Defer any retirement income you have as long as you can to reap the maximum benefits.

• If you can, wait as long as possible to collect your Social Security benefits so that you will receive the maximum amount for which you are eligible. David waited until he was seventy to retire and, as a result, receives $2,000 a month from Social Security.

• Allow yourself to dream about the different work opportunities you can explore. Whether you want to start a business, hang out a consulting shingle, or work part-time for a company, believe that anything is possible. Does the world discriminate against older people in the workforce? Of course. Your objective, however, is to find that niche for yourself where discrimination won't affect you.

• Do much of the legwork and planning for your new work venture *before* you retire. Give yourself a reasonable amount of time to learn about what you need to know and to do.

• Check out *www.2young2retire.com* for ideas about reinventing retirement for yourself. This site offers tips, tools, and stories about how to gain a fresh perspective on your "postcareer" life, whether it be a new career or business, volunteer or nonprofit work, going back to school or learning something new.

• Get a clean bill of health. Make appointments with all of your doctors, including your internist, dentist, dermatologist, gynecologist, and any other specialists.

Use the following questions to plan your retirement:

1. Do you have a financial planner with whom you feel comfortable?

_____

_____

_____

2. If not, when will you begin getting referrals and interviewing financial planners?

_____

_____

_____

3. Are there geographic locations that you are interested in relocating to? What are they?

_____

_____

_____

4. Have you investigated them thoroughly? If not, when do you plan on doing so?

_____

_____

_____

5. If you are working now, when do you plan on leaving your job?

_____

_____

_____

6. Have you thought about the kind of work you'd like to do when you leave your current position? If so, what is it?

_____

_____

_____

7. What steps do you plan on taking to create new work or find your next job?

_____

_____

_____

Remember that this next phase in your life should be fun, interesting, fulfilling, illuminating, and exhilarating! In an article written in 2000, Lydia Bronte, a senior fellow at the Hunter College Brookdale Center on Aging, commented, "Some people find their best fit career-wise after the age of fifty and some, even more surprisingly, after the age of sixty-five. People need to keep in mind that the best part of your career may still be ahead of you."

Jerry is a great example of this. After working in multiple careers that included the Navy, consumer product sales, executive search and outplacement, Jerry, at sixty-eight, is retired from the corporate world. He started his own small company, which provides career transition seminars for flag rank (admirals and generals) military, counseling and retention classes at the Naval War College in Newport, Rhode Island, and other career management services for junior naval officers. He feels so blessed that at the end of a series of successful careers, he has been able to create work for himself that he loves and excels at. Jerry says, "I feel that my background in management as well as the need to 'do good' have prepared me for the work I'm doing, which has real meaning. I'm away from corporate politics, although I miss the social interaction. As long as God gives me the health and the credibility, I plan on continuing to contribute as long as possible, perhaps ratcheting down a bit at a time. This year I'll work about ten percent less than last year, but I get paid real well for what I do, and I have a modest Navy Reserve retirement and also now collect Social Security."

Len, sixty-five, sold his bread distribution business when he was sixty-two. An avid fisherman and hunter, he wanted a flexible schedule, so he went to work for a limousine service in central Florida, where he drives people to and from the airport. While he enjoys meeting new people every day, he's beginning to feel that his employer is too dependent on him. Because of this, Len has decided to find another type of part-time work. He loves the fact that he can keep trying different kinds of work, something he couldn't do easily when he was supporting his family by working in his own business.

Retirement can and should be an interesting and fulfilling phase in your life. It is an ideal time to experiment with different kinds of work without the stress and pressures that you may have experienced in your career. As a 2001 AARP ad says, "Age is just a number, and life is what you make of it."

CHAPTER 11

The Ten Keys to Success

In his best-selling book *Emotional Intelligence,* Daniel Goleman writes, "There are widespread exceptions to the rule that IQ predicts success—at best, IQ contributes about 20% to the factors that determine life success, which leaves 80% to other forces." Goleman goes on to explain, "These other characteristics are called emotional intelligence: abilities such as being able to motivate oneself and persist in the face of frustrations; to control impulse and delay gratification; to regulate one's moods and keep distress from swamping the ability to think; to empathize and to hope."

This book is full of assessments, tools, resources, and how-tos to help guide you in finding new work that will better meet your personal and financial needs. No matter which category you fit within, however, unless you are able to demonstrate and master a very specific set of life skills and traits, you will find it very difficult to be successful in finding the work you want.

"The Ten Keys to Success" come from intuitive observations of and experience with people in the workplace. Time and again, it is apparent that those individuals who exhibit these ten keys and use them most productively are consistently the more successful and well-liked individuals overall. The good news is that most people are born with at least some of these keys or learned them at a very young age, and all of these keys can be developed or learned later in life.

The Ten Keys to Success are:

1. Curiosity: being eager to know and learn; always showing interest and giving special attention to the less obvious; always being the person who says," I want to know more about . . ."
2. Decisiveness: arriving at a final conclusion or making a choice and taking action: making decisions with determination, even when you don't have all of the information you think you need.
3. Perseverance: having passion, energy, focus, and the desire to get results. Motivation, persistence, and hard work are all aspects of drive.
4. Empathy: demonstrating caring and understanding of someone else's situation, feelings, and motives; always thinking about what it's like to walk in someone else's shoes.
5. Flexibility: being capable of change; responding positively to change; being pliable, adaptable, nonrigid, and able to deal with ambiguity.
6. Follow-through: always closing the loop and taking the next step; honoring your word by doing what you said you would do and being professional in your communication and approach.
7. Humor: viewing yourself and the world with enjoyment; not taking life or yourself too seriously; being amusing, amused, and, at times, even comical.
8. Intelligence: thinking and working smartly and cleverly; being sharp in your dealings; "not reinventing the wheel"; planning before acting; working efficiently and focusing on

quality over quantity. (Important note: This is different from IQ, the common abbreviation for intelligence quotient.)

9. Optimism: expecting the best possible outcome and dwelling on the most hopeful or positive aspects of a situation; subscribing to the belief that "the glass is half full" rather than "half empty."

10. Respect: remembering that it's just as easy to be nice; protecting another person's self-esteem; treating others in a considerate and courteous manner.

Which of these keys are among your strengths? Which of the ten are among your weaknesses? Self-awareness—the ability to recognize a feeling as it happens—is really the foundation for understanding yourself. If you are not sure how self-aware you are, ask several people whom you trust which of these ten keys they believe are your strengths, and which are not. Again, while no one person possesses all ten of these keys in equal amounts, each of them can be developed and improved.

Curiosity

Are you curious? Do you constantly seek to learn about new ideas and gather new information, no matter what the topic? Or are you only concerned with learning about and knowing just what interests you? When you meet a new person, do you really make an effort to get to know him or her, or are many of your encounters superficial in nature?

We all have an unlimited potential for learning. We can also hold ourselves back from learning by allowing certain fears, such as the fear of failure or a fear of success, to inhibit us. Sometimes, we may let a lack of training or experience keep us from being inquisitive and interested in new things. The trouble with this approach is that being curious and learning about people, jobs, and business is extremely necessary to the process of finding satisfying work. Our natural tendency is to believe that we must be interested in something before we are willing to learn more about it. Yet, at times, we surprise ourselves by becoming interested in something we didn't think we cared about.

Jonathan had the courage to leave a secure job at a *Fortune* 50 company in order to seek a more rewarding and challenging career and to balance his family life, which included his newborn daughter. He hired a career counselor who helped him define his unique strengths, skills, passions, and hidden talents. He honed his curiosity by networking in new areas of business, attending trade shows, and exploring areas he had never been exposed to directly. Jonathan read new books, listened to audiocassettes, and attended presentations about career change. All of the new information he absorbed really opened his eyes to the career possibilities that existed for him. He started his own company doing business strategy and due diligence, and leads a very balanced life that includes participating in his daughter's life and spending time on his boat, things he'd never be able to do if he still worked for the *Fortune* 50 company.

When you are curious and interested in learning from others, it shows. Constantly asking questions of the people you meet and really listening to their answers during the process of exploring new career situations and opportunities—as well as in your other social interactions, both formal and informal—are great ways to develop your curiosity. Becoming a better listener will help you to become more curious and interested. Really focusing intently on what people are saying, without jumping to immediate conclusions, will enable you to learn and understand information more easily. Trying to understand and learn about people's motives, feelings, and emotions—not just facts— is important as well.

Decisiveness

Making decisions is a crucial part of changing your work. One of the reasons so many people remain in an unhappy or unsatisfying job situation is because they simply can't make any decisions. The trouble with this is that without decisions, there are no results! Decisions are based upon gathering as much information as possible without getting stuck in a state of "analysis paralysis." Involving the people who are affected by your decisions, such as your advisers or your family, is also a meaningful part of making decisions. Your intuition—that is, what your "gut," "inner voice," or "sixth sense" tells you to do—is another significant element of decision-making. Balancing these three components can be a challenge, and making a decision, let alone making the one that's best for you, is often not that simple.

It's also very important to remember that there is no perfect decision. Deciding finally to do something about being unhappy with your work is one of the hardest decisions that you can make in life. But once you make the first decision to change your work, continuing to make the small decisions you need to make along the way will not only make you feel better but will also become easier.

If you can't make a decision easily, ask yourself what the worst possible outcome could be. Rarely does the worst possible scenario ever happen, but even if it does, ask yourself what you would do if it did, and how you could turn it around.

How can you be more decisive? If you follow this simple thought process when making a decision, it will become much easier.

1. Define a specific problem or situation with your work. Try to focus on the actual problem, not just the symptoms.
2. Decide what it is that you want to achieve. In other words,

what do you want the immediate outcome of your decision to be? What about the long-term outcome?

3. Consider your options.

4. Do you have all the information you need to make the decision? If not, and the information is accessible, getting the information will make the decision a lot easier for you. You can use the formula journalists use by asking yourself: who? what? where? when? why? and how? If you have all this information, there should be no reason not to make the decision.

5. Do you have to make this decision alone? While so much of the process of finding satisfying work comes from you, there is no need to do it alone. Consult with people who are supportive of you and people who are experts, or at least knowledgeable about you and your situation.

6. How have you handled similar issues in the past? If you haven't had to make decisions related to your career in the past, find out how other people have done so. It's time to learn how to make this an easier and more comfortable process.

7. Do you have a track record of making poor decisions? If so, why? Is there something you can change about how you make decisions?

8. Do you rely too heavily on other people's input? Everyone has an opinion, whether you ask for it or not. Sift through this information and use what makes sense for you.

9. Is there someone whose style of decision-making you admire? Can you spend some time with that person to learn how they make decisions?

10. If you were to set a timer for a half hour, what would your immediate decision be about what to do next regarding your career?

In making decisions, be willing to take risks, and to forgive yourself if you make a decision that doesn't turn out to be the right one for you.

Darleen started a candy business with her husband, and after working in the business for five years—every one of which was miserable—she admitted that opening the business was a mistake. Once she faced the fact that the decision to operate the candy business wasn't a good one, she made another decision to cut her losses, sold her candy business, and started a technology training business. Running the candy business had been a painful experience, and unfortunately it took Darleen a long time to decide to do something about closing it and starting a different type of business. But she did make a change and she's never been happier.

Gene left a successful career in the construction business to go to law school. With a wife and three children to consider, he was not sure how he would make it work. When he was thinking about taking the plunge, he said, "At some point I realized that the *only* thing that stood between me and a law degree was simply the decision to do it." When Gene described his decision-making process, he said, "I like to make decisions that have inherent guarantees of success. That does not mean risk is to be avoided. To the contrary, you can embrace risk if you focus your energy on breaking down any barriers to success. In the decision-making process that I engaged in, I simply identified all the barriers and then sought a way to overcome each barrier."

Perseverance

Steve Mariucci, the San Francisco 49ers head coach, said, "I never wear a watch, because I always know it's now—and now is when you should do it."

Without perseverance, you will not achieve at the highest levels. It is necessary for goal-setting, learning, developing and nurturing relationships, and maintaining momentum. Changing careers requires an extraordinary amount of energy and motivation, and perseverance encompasses these two things, as well as focus and the desire for results. For the most part, motivation comes from inside yourself: your thoughts, your behavior, and your attitudes.

Maria received her master's degree in teaching English as a second language at the age of fifty-four. She had always gravitated toward business situations that were new and nonestablished and believes that "drive pushes us toward uncharted territory, but eventually we decide to stop and develop what we've learned into something." In Maria's case, she designed a program for Japanese nationals on how to live and conduct business when they are sent to the United States as staff for American branches of Japanese companies. Without perseverance, Maria would not have been able to successfully create her new business. She was motivated, focused, and passionate about learning what the Japanese nationals needed and creating the right program.

How can you develop perseverance? The first step is to feel passionate about your goals, about the career you have or the one you are trying to move into. Passion is very personal, and you will only feel it if what you are investigating and moving toward is right for you. If you are pursuing someone else's idea of what you should be doing, it will be nearly impossible for you to feel passionate.

Setting very specific activity goals during every phase of your search for satisfying work is a must, even for the introspective and soul-searching phase. Goals represent your purpose and the outcome you wish to achieve. Even the most motivated person will lag in his or her efforts at times without goals to work toward. Keep your goals simple, measurable, and realistic.

Find someone else who is going through a similar situation with his or her work, and agree to partner with this person in your individual searches for new work. Set up a healthy but competitive relationship to compare notes and coach each other along toward accomplishing your goals. Goals you might set for each other could include completing research on a specific industry by a specific deadline and scheduling a specific number of informational meetings. When you are held accountable in this friendly yet competitive way, you will be motivated much more than if you set goals on your own and share them with no one.

Without physical energy, you will be unable to maintain a high level of motivation for long. Keep your energy level high by staying healthy, working out, eating properly, and taking vitamins. Take time off regularly during your quest for new and satisfying work and keep your mental, emotional, and spiritual health intact. Hire a feng shui expert or an organizational consultant to help you streamline or reorganize your work environment. Think of statements or phrases that you can say to yourself to motivate you when you aren't feeling positive or focused—things like "I can do this" or "All I need to do to keep going is . . ."

Stefanie, an independent consultant in private practice with her husband, says after having several successful careers as a psychologist, the manager of an outplacement office, and an entrepreneur, "I have huge respect for perseverance as a quality." She knows that "Talent goes nowhere without perseverance. It has been a key ingredient in my career. I had the perseverance to get my Ph.D., and to get licensed; to get promoted to run an office; to run a successful and profitable office for my employer; and to run a successful consulting practice as an entrepreneur."

Empathy

According to Daniel Goleman, empathy builds on self-awareness. This means that the more in tune we are to ourselves and our emotions, the more skilled we will be in reading someone else's feelings. Your capacity or ability to know or intuit how someone else feels is key to successful interactions with others in your career discovery process. Goleman says, "The key to intuiting another's feelings is in the ability to read nonverbal channels:

tone of voice, gesture, facial expression, and the like." He goes on to say that "the benefits of being able to read feelings from nonverbal cues include being better adjusted emotionally, more popular, more outgoing, and—perhaps not surprisingly—more sensitive." Your ability to understand and read other people will greatly increase your comfort level with the process of discovering work that will fulfill your needs. Being empathic toward others will sharpen your insights about what makes people thrive and be happy in their work. You can then more easily relate these insights to your own needs and desires regarding finding new work.

There are several simple things you can do to enhance your empathy toward others:

- Ask questions and really listen to the answers.
- Respond to the answers with additional well-thought-out questions.
- Respond to body language, facial expressions, and eye contact.
- Try to understand what other people are thinking and feeling, and what may be motivating them.
- Whenever you start thinking about yourself, immediately refocus your attention on the other person.

Jonathan, who left the *Fortune* 50 company to search for a new career, didn't focus on his own needs. When he realized how challenging and emotionally charged a job search can be, he started investing his time in meeting and coaching other unemployed individuals who had been downsized or let go. He found that by volunteering his time to offer advice and hope to others, he became more empathic in his own career quest. As he found himself becoming more interested in other people and less focused on himself, his interactions with other people were more meaningful during his job search.

Flexibility

It can be rather difficult to pursue a new career or a new type of work without being flexible. You may prefer more structure and, as a result, you may favor following a routine that enables you to know where you will be and what you will be doing most of the time. Unfortunately, such a predictable lifestyle is difficult to achieve through the many phases of looking for gratifying work.

During this process, you will be initiating conversations and having meetings with people you've never met before or don't know well. Any of these individuals may give you a new or different idea or piece of information that could be very useful to you. Being open to the unexpected is important. Saying things like "I would never do that" will make you appear rigid to other people and could deter them from offering helpful information to you.

The quest for new work usually presents constant change and ambiguity. Learning to cope with these challenges can be difficult; however, if you choose not to deal with them in a positive way or to completely resist them, you will find that your attitude will negatively color other people's perceptions of you.

Maria, the self-employed ESL instructor and consultant, admits that she is not very flexible emotionally. Although she is constantly seeking the new, the unknown, and the next challenge, at the same time she loves the comfort of the secure and the predictable. This presents a true conflict for Maria. The way she deals with this conflict is by automatically asking herself if she is being flexible in her approach, communication, and attitude.

Follow-through

By following through on something, you are taking action and moving it forward. Because your quest for satisfying work is so dependent upon the people you meet and the relationships you develop and nurture, it is crucial to do everything in your power to remain memorable to everyone you meet. Sending a handwritten note, a postcard, or an e-mail; leaving a voice mail message; or scheduling another meeting are great ways to do this.

An important component of networking and interviewing is reciprocity—that is, your ability to offer to help the person you are talking to so that the relationship will be more evenly balanced and mutually productive. This means that if you have promised to do something, you should honor your word and do it. Follow-through should be consistently planned. It should become second nature and a top priority!

Humor

Humor can relieve the stress of the seemingly monumental process you are thinking of undertaking. There are so many times, situations, and circumstances during your search for gratifying work when a chuckle or a good laugh is all you'll need to shift your mood or change your outlook from negative to positive.

Daniel Goleman explains that happiness can actually cause physiological changes in the human brain as well as in our overall physical and psychological well-being. Happiness, he says, can bring about "an increased activity that inhibits negative feelings and fosters an increase in available energy, and a quieting of those feelings that generate worrisome thought.

This configuration offers the body a general rest, as well as readiness and enthusiasm for whatever task is at hand and for striving toward a variety of goals."

A scientific explanation for this phenomenon is that laughter, which typically results from humor, stimulates endorphins in the brain, which in turn decreases physical or emotional pain. Hopefully, you won't experience too much—or any—pain during this process! At times, though, you will feel discomfort, uneasiness, or other unpleasant emotions that humor and its by-product—laughter—will relieve.

How can you generate and sustain humor?

- Keep a progressive record of your career-search journey, writing down the humorous moments that occur.
- If you are experiencing stress, learn to view your experiences from an amusing perspective.
- Nurture your sense of humor by going to a comedy club, renting funny movies, and reading humorous books.
- Try to surround yourself with upbeat, smiling, happy, and lighthearted individuals. Humor is contagious!

Intelligence

Intelligence is about thinking and working smart, realizing where your intelligence lies and taking advantage of other people's intelligence as well. While your specific career situation is very personal, remember that there are innumerable people in the world who have already experienced the same things you are going through. These people have created new work, changed careers, started and bought businesses, and accomplished everything that is discussed in this book. Intelligence is finding a handful of people who have been in the same boat and learning from their mistakes and successes.

Christina is in her late thirties and has changed careers four times already. She worked in investment banking and then became an independent event planner. She then worked as an independent contractor, before moving into her current job running the North American operation of a global network of health managers. When asked for an example of how she demonstrated intelligence in her career changing, she said, "It is very important to develop or improve skills that you will need during the process of changing careers. At the same time, I believe that we are all good at many things and less good at other things, and we shouldn't waste our time devoting energy away from the good stuff, especially since the 'good stuff' is usually what we like best anyway."

This means that if it isn't fun or productive to reinvent the wheel while moving through the process of reshaping your work, seek out someone who already has and ask them to share their findings with you.

Optimism

This particular quality gets a lot of attention in the world today. Deservedly so! If I had to choose three keys of the ten that are the most basic to your success in the pursuit of satisfying work, I'd say that optimism is one of them, the other two being perseverance and curiosity. Keith Harrell, whose clients are primarily downsized workers, is the author of the book *Attitude Is Everything*. He believes, "Life is not what happens to you, it's what you do about it."

Martin Seligman, Ph.D., the author of *Learned Optimism,* says, "Optimistic people feel that good things will last a long time and will have a beneficial effect on everything they do. They think that bad things are isolated: They won't last too long and won't affect other parts of life."

In a September 2000 *Health* magazine article, Judith Newman wrote about Seligman's theory: "Most fundamentally, this perspective reflects how much control you think you have over your life—a sense of control may be the single most important trait that distinguishes the Little Engines That Could of the world from the woe-is-me Eeyore types."

Seligman says, "Positive thinkers feel powerful and negative thinkers feel helpless because they have been conditioned to believe that they're screwed no matter what."

Take this brief quiz to see how you score as a positive person. Circle the answer that most describes you.

1. You arrive at the airport only to find out you've missed your flight because your car service was twenty minutes late picking you up and you hit traffic on the way.
   A. You yell at the ticket agent and demand that he get you on the next flight *and* put you in first class.
   B. You politely inquire which flight is the next one to leave and then smile and say, "I had a few phone calls to make anyway."

2. You're about to give a major presentation to some senior executives at your company, and five minutes before you're scheduled to start, you can't get the LCD projector to turn on.
   A. You mutter loudly under your breath, "Goddammit, this always happens to me. When is technology ever going to work?"
   B. You announce to the group that you really think that your presentation has more impact without the PowerPoint slides and plan to begin in two minutes if everyone is ready.

3. Your boss sits down with you and tells you that he's very sorry but that he is going to have to let you go as part of a big organizational budget-cutting initiative.
   A. You react angrily and tell him that you'll never find another job at your same level of compensation and hope he feels good about ruining your career.
   B. You take a deep breath and say, "Well, this is a bit of a

shock, so when I feel calmer I'd like to meet with you to discuss arrangements for my separation package."

4. You've finally decided to explore a new field after taking some diagnostic tests and doing research. During your first networking meeting, the person you are talking to casually mentions that it's a tough field to break into.

A. You go home and tell your spouse that you'll never get hired in the new industry and maybe you'd better just look for another job in your current field.

B. You ask your networking contact what advice she would give you about the things you can do to ease your entry into the field.

5. You're been recruiting and interviewing candidates for three months for a key position in your department. You finally find the ideal candidate and, just as you're about to make her an offer, your boss tells you that he's decided not to increase the head count in your department for this fiscal year.

A. Frustrated, you become emotional and tell your boss that he's making your job impossible to do, and that you'll never hit your business goals without this new person on board.

B. You ask your boss if you can sit down with him and have a planning meeting about ways that you can utilize other resources within your company to help you accomplish your objectives for the year. You also make an effort to stay in touch with the candidates in the hope that eventually the head count situation will turn around.

SCORE KEY

Needless to say, if you did (or really wanted to) select any "A" answers, these are not the approaches an optimist would take.

Optimism is said to be genetically predisposed; however, research has shown that environment and life experiences have just as much to do with one's tendency toward optimism. It has been proven, too, that optimism can be learned.

How can you become more optimistic?

• Whenever something negative or difficult happens, ask yourself what you've learned from your experience. Write this down so that the next time something similar happens, you're better prepared to handle it.

• If you are thinking about something in a negative way, distract yourself immediately by remembering an incident that made you laugh recently, or by thinking about how you can relax over the weekend.

• It's easy to be negative if you're feeling overwhelmed. The best way to stop feeling overwhelmed is to think of everything in small steps and little pieces. What is the one thing you can do today to move toward accomplishing your goals?

• Immediately call or e-mail the most positive person you know and ask him or her to help you reframe your negative thoughts.

• Exercise. Get some fresh air. Try a new yoga class. Do something—anything—physical to change your perspective and get those endorphins flowing! The Mayo Clinic conducted a study in the year 2000 that compared the health of more than eight hundred men and women to their scores on a personality test they had taken thirty years earlier. Those individuals who tested high on the optimism scale years ago were 19 percent more likely to be alive than their less optimistic fellow test-takers.

• Focus on the positive aspect of your life, no matter how small: the clean bill of health you recently received from your doctor, your new haircut, the golf outing you have planned with your buddies, the big bouquet of tulips you brought for yourself, or the e-mail you just received from your old college friend.

Respect

My father is fond of saying, "It's just as easy to be nice." Being pleasant and gracious to everyone without exception, using good manners by always saying "Please," "Thank you," and "Excuse me" and complimenting others so they feel good about themselves are all the basics of respect.

You may be thinking, "Isn't this pretty obvious stuff?" Well, yes, it should be; however, we all know people who don't routinely exhibit respectful behavior to others.

Rosenbluth International, a Philadelphia-based global travel services company, actually looks for and hires candidates who are "nice." Rosenbluth has made *Fortune* magazine's 100 Best Companies to Work For in America, in part because of their effort to attract employees who share the same values, one of which is caring.

In your interactions with other people during the course of your pursuit for fulfilling work, being conscious of how considerate you are will improve your overall success.

If during your search for satisfying work, you feel stymied or frustrated, review the Ten Keys to Success. If you focus on them, you will remain grounded and secure in the knowledge that you can make the changes you need to find satisfying work!

CHAPTER 12

Job Search—the Nuts and Bolts

Your Job Search

In 1999, Richard Bolles was interviewed by *Fast Company* magazine about his perspective on what has changed about finding a job since he first wrote *What Color Is Your Parachute?* in 1970. The more important question, Bolles pointed out, was what had remained constant. And his answer? "Human nature. It doesn't change and people don't like rejection, they never have and never will."

At times during your search, you may feel overwhelmed, frustrated, intimidated, uncomfortable, insecure, rejected, and/or depressed. Experiencing any of these emotions is completely normal. Some people you will encounter will be arrogant or insensitive, or behave unprofessionally. This, too, is normal. On the positive side, there will be times when you are likely to feel euphoric, hopeful, excited, and self-confident. In fact, your job search process may amplify such positive emotions to the point where you'll wish that you could "bottle" them. Many of the people whom you will talk to or meet with will be kind, professional, complimentary, and optimistic about your chances of landing the job or work situation of your dreams. You should expect some, or many, of these behaviors and reactions "to come with the territory" as you pursue the search for work that you love.

Now that you know where you are and where you want to be in your career, here are some tools that you can use while you are looking for a job. Regardless of the condition of the job market or how great an influence technology may have on the workplace, certain fundamental truths about the process of looking for a job will always remain the same.

Relationships Are Essential to Changing Jobs

The harder you work at nurturing your existing relationships, developing new ones and revitalizing old ones, the easier and more rewarding the job search process will be for you. A relationship is not someone on a list of contacts with whom you have no real connection. A relationship involves interaction between two people in which there is consistent communication, the individuals involved are familiar with each other's work and perhaps even their life situation, trust exists, and both people are interested in helping the other. It's a bonus when the two people in the relationship share common interests or goals, and really like each other. Since relationships require a great deal of hard work, many people just aren't willing to do what is necessary to create and cultivate them. Regardless of whether or not you are conducting a job search, part of your work should always be creating new relationships and nurturing the ones you have.

What if you've let go of many of your relationships because you've buried yourself in your work? Contrary to what many people think, it's easier and makes more sense to rekindle the relationships you've let go of than to go out and try to develop new ones. The person you've had a relationship with in the past already knows you, so trust and rapport can be reignited more easily. If you haven't talked with someone in a while, it's always interesting to hear about what's changed in that person's life and work situation. She may have been wondering about you and feeling uncomfortable because she, too, hasn't done much lately to foster your relationship, and now you've done the hard part by getting in touch with her first. People inherently like to be helpful to others, and are more inclined to do so with someone they already know.

New relationships are also very important in a successful job search. Ask your existing friends and acquaintances for referrals to people they know with whom you can talk. Since people tend to respond to someone they don't know if the introduction is made through someone they do, make sure to acknowledge the person whom you have in common. When beginning a new relationship, it's important to communicate that although you obviously are seeking their assistance, you are also approaching them to begin a mutually fulfilling relationship. This means that well after you are settled in your new job or career, you should continue to nurture these new relationships.

You Must Know Yourself

The clearer you are about your preferences, likes and dislikes, strengths and weaknesses—the essence of who you are—the more straightforward your job search process will be. By now, you have gone over your self-assessments several times and have a clear sense of who you are and what you want. If you don't, go back to the chapters that describe your situation and review your self-assessments.

When you are ready to launch your job search, it is essential that you are able to tell other people, both orally and in writing, who you are, how this translates to what you are looking for, and how you can contribute and make a difference in the work you are pursuing. Often, people in the heat of a job search have great difficulty articulating their interests or the ways that they made improvements in previous jobs. Instead, the nervous interviewee tends to talk only about his or her present or past job tasks, responsibilities, and skills. This tendency, coupled with the likelihood that the person doing the interviewing may not be a skilled interviewer, can be a recipe for an unsuccessful job interview.

How can you prepare this information?

1. Think about an accomplishment you achieved in a previous job by answering these questions:

   What was an obstacle, challenge, or situation that needed to be changed or improved in your job?

   _____

   _____

   _____

   _____

   Fred, a human resources manager, noticed that employee turnover on the hourly levels was very high.

   What did you do to change or improve it?

   _____

   _____

   _____

   _____

   Fred began surveying hourly workers about their working conditions and the reasons they were dissatisfied. He then asked them for suggestions for ways to make their work more satisfactory. Using this information, Fred created a program just for hourly workers that encompassed small bonuses for meeting goals, flextime, and an allowance for technical education, and he turned an unused conference room into an employee lounge.

What was the result of the changes you made? (Use quantifiable measurements if you can, like percentages and numbers.)

_____

_____

_____

_____

Fred began tracking the hourly employee turnover rate, which went from 80 percent before he started the program to 55 percent six months after the program was in place.

2. Write down your accomplishment in one succinct sentence.

_____

_____

_____

_____

Fred can say, "I reduced hourly employee turnover from 80 percent to 55 percent, by implementing a special program which motivated and rewarded hourly workers."

3. Identify three accomplishments for each job you've held, including your current position, and write them down. Practice this below:

What was an obstacle, challenge, or situation that needed to be changed or improved in your job?

_____

_____

_____

_____

What did you do to change or improve it? (Use quantifiable mea-
surements if you can, like percentages and numbers.)

_____

_____

_____

_____

What was the result of the changes you made?

_____

_____

_____

_____

Have a Focused and Flexible Plan with Realistic, Achievable Goals

Having a written, focused, and flexible plan, which includes specific action steps for achieving your goals and objectives, will help ensure that you will reach your destination. A plan will also help you avoid wasting time doing things that are counterproductive.

It is ironic that when we embark upon something as meaningful as looking for a job or changing careers, we rarely put a large amount of effort into planning and goal-setting. Although this may be because we lack the motivation or the skills to plan, it is usually because of a psychological mind-set that accompanies our approach to the job search. Too often, we become overwhelmed by the task, and yet, a plan can and should be simple, specific, and flexible, with goals that are realistic, quantifiable, and small. Here's an example: Sam said he wanted a senior marketing or operations position within the consumer products industry. He wanted to secure this new career within six months and was determined to find it by actively networking with everyone he had ever met. He set the realistic goal for himself of talking with two people every week about his plan. Sam's criterion for identifying people was anyone who he felt was approachable, liked him, knew a lot of other people, or actually worked in consumer products. Using this criterion, he was able to create a long list of people. Within three months, he landed a marketing executive position in New Jersey, working for an old college friend.

You should always write down your plan. Here is a sample:

My Job Search   Week of_____
My three primary goals are:

1. Finish my résumé and show it to three people for feedback.

   Did I do this?   *Yes*   *No*
   Notes:

   _____

   _____

   _____

   _____

2. Make a list of fifteen people to contact with their phone numbers and e-mail addresses.

Did I do this?   *Yes*   *No*
Notes:

_____

_____

_____

_____

3. Call five people on this list with the goal of setting up a face-to-face meeting with each one.

Did I do this?   *Yes*   *No*
Notes:

_____

_____

_____

_____

Save your plans each week, keeping them in one place so that you can refer to them if you need to.

You Must Make Decisions and Take Action

A plan is essential, but if you fail to make decisions, or to act upon the decisions you do make, your job search will be futile. Decisions drive action. Without action—making phone calls, following up those calls, setting up meetings, and scheduling interviews—it is impossible to find a new job or make the changes you'd like to make in your work. The inability to make decisions can stem from many things, including insecurity, lack of passion, and fear: fear of success, fear of failure, and fear of change or the unknown. The irony is that taking action and experiencing success is the best possible remedy for overcoming fear and vanquishing insecurity. As for not having passion, this means that either you are pursuing something that you think you should do, or that someone else wants for you, or you simply don't have enough information. We humans just don't make decisions if we aren't motivated to do so. Learning what your motivation is, is the first step to making decisions.

Harold, a vice president of training, hired a career coach because he had no passion for his career and, at age forty, was feeling inordinately dissatisfied and unhappy. In his first meeting with his coach, Harold told her that his biggest problem, in his view, was that he was incapable of making decisions. He had changed careers twice in the past but did so easily because people he knew brought him into those jobs at a time in his life when he was younger and more flexible. Since then, he had pursued careers in law, advertising, and the nonprofit sector. In each instance, he had been made an offer or was set to embark on the next step, when he became paralyzed about making a decision that would move him into a new career.

Harold began to make a plan every week enabling him to make small decisions about researching industries, networking with people, answering Internet ads, and finding opportunities. He experienced a lot of highs and lows during his search, but a year and a half later, he did find a job with a public relations firm. He credits his success to getting into the habit of asking himself, "What's the next decision I need to make about my job search?" until making decisions became habitual for Harold and no longer an obstacle.

The Most Important Elements of a Job Search

Your Résumé

The first thing that many people think about when deciding to embark on a job search is writing a résumé. Most companies still rely on résumés to learn about a candidate's work history and use it as a tool when interviewing. Another reason for knowing who you are, what you want, and what you have to offer is so you can put this information on your résumé. Although a résumé serves as documentation of your career history, it has three even more important purposes:

1. Writing a good résumé requires you to spend quality time thinking about who you are and the impact you've made in the past. Once you've done this, it will be much easier for you to handle face-to-face discussions with a networking contact or interviewer.

2. You can creatively describe your experiences and accomplishments in a way that can effectively match the interviewer's needs.

3. The opportunity to express your unique personality traits and skills on paper can help you to distinguish yourself from other candidates.

Writing a résumé for the Internet is a different process from writing your résumé for a human being to hold in his or her hands. There are hundreds of thousands of jobs listed on the Internet, and you'll need to create an on-line-compatible résumé with keywords in a different text form in order to post it. While the Internet is a powerful and ubiquitous tool for you to use in your job search, ultimately a human being will be sitting in a room with you, reading your résumé. So creating two versions is a good idea. Some difference between an online résumé and a traditional résumé are:

ON-LINE RÉSUMÉ	TRADITIONAL RÉSUMÉ
Noun-heavy with a focus on keywords. For example, keywords might be *Java, nonprofit, purchasing, consumer products,* and *human resources.* These key words are usually placed at the beginning or the end of your résumé, rather than the middle.	Verb-heavy with a focus on action. Examples of action verbs are *succeeded, originated, devised, created,* and *managed.*
Focus is on describing a specific job in your career history, one that's closest to the job you are applying for.	Organized from a chronological standpoint, listing all the jobs you've had in your career.
Should be as simple and plain as possible without unusual fonts or graphic elements.	Can be more creatively designed with different typefaces and spacing.
Can be any length, but typos are even more glaring when picked up by a scanner.	No longer than two pages, and typos aren't acceptable on this version either.

Your résumé represents you and is often what people use to assess you even before you meet. Because of this, you should write the best résumé possible. On the other hand, spending more time writing your résumé than planning your job search strategy will not be the best use of your time.

Networking

Networking will always be an important part of the job search process, so you should become comfortable with it. Learning to network is analogous to learning how to ride a bicycle. When you were little, it seemed so impossible to learn to ride a two-wheeler. But once you learned how, it was exhilarating at first, and then it became second nature. Now, you can't imagine not being able to remember how to ride a bike. Even if you've gone a while without riding one, you will feel a bit wobbly at first, but then you will hit your familiar stride.

Fear of the unknown is perfectly normal. Being fearful of unpleasant experiences is normal, too. If you are fearful of networking, the best way to handle your anxiety is to think of the worst possible scenario. Ask yourself, "What's the worst that could happen?" Chances are, your fear will be harder to deal with than the actual negative or unpleasant outcome that might result from your taking a risk. If you are fearful of being rejected, remind yourself that it is unlikely someone will reject you as a person in a networking situation. They may not take the time to talk with or meet you because they either don't know how to help you, or they don't see the value in it. Since there are so many people who do engage in networking, it makes sense just to move on if you are getting either a negative response or no response from a particular individual.

Here are some ways to begin the networking process:

1. Make a list of everyone you know, dividing them into categories such as professional services, neighbors, former business colleagues, friends, and college alumni. You will be continually surprised by the people who will help you during your networking process, like your dentist or neighbor three doors down.

2. It is ideal if you purchase contact management software such as Act! or Outlook to keep your network organized. Whether or not you do this, be sure to keep all the names and contact information in one place.

3. Before you e-mail or call anyone on your list, write a brief script stating what it is you're looking for. Be specific and succinct. Your script will have an introduction, something like: "I can't believe it's been two years since we've talked, how are you

doing?" Then describe what you're doing in one or two sentences: "I'm calling you because I've decided to make a career change and I had heard that you did the same thing about a year ago." The last part of the script discusses a next step: "I'd be so appreciative if we could spend twenty minutes together to that you can share your experience with me. When would this be convenient for you?"

4. Come to the networking meeting prepared with a résumé (if appropriate), a business card (even if you are unemployed, have simple business cards printed with your name and contact information), and knowing what two or three pieces of information you are looking for. Are you looking for feedback on your résumé or the names of people at a specific company? If you don't do this, the information you gather may not be useful to you.

5. Always ask the person if there is anything you can do to help them. They could be looking for a new baby-sitter or trying to buy a new car and you may be able to help him or her as well.

6. Your networking style is crucial. The impression you make really matters. Be sure that you look and sound professional and confident. Don't ramble on and on about yourself.

7. Any gathering of people presents an opportunity for you to network. Baseball games, association meetings, your neighborhood block party, and the grocery store are all full of people who know what's going on in the business world and know other people.

8. Always send a thank-you note or e-mail to the person immediately after your meeting. Tell them that you plan on staying in touch with them periodically. You should initiate follow-up, particularly if he or she has offered to send you someone's name or other information.

Networking is a life skill, not just something you do when you are changing jobs. The more you practice it, the more useful it will become to you, not only during your time of transition, but even when you are happily working.

Answering Internet or Newspaper Ads

While both newspaper and Internet ads are very useful job search tools, they are no longer the primary way to get a job, and haven't been for quite a while. Companies today are becoming much more creative in their approaches to recruiting new employees— placing ads on buses and subways, in public bathrooms, or even on trash cans, for example. Many offer financially rewarding referral programs for existing employees with links on their company Web sites that list descriptions of current job openings. By all means, answer ads if you'd like, keeping in mind that this conventional method is not the most warm, interactive, or multidimensional way to communicate with a potential employer.

Contingency and Search Firms

Contingency firms are used by companies to find candidates in a specific salary range—usually under $100,000. They don't normally sign a contract with the company for whom they are recruiting candidates, and are only paid a fee when a candidate is hired. Search (or retainer) firms are used by companies for filling senior level positions, typically those that pay $100,000 or more. Search firms sign an agreement and receive their fee in installments, even if they never find a candidate who is hired by the company.

Both types of firms have one client—the company that hires them. Most of the time, if you are a job candidate who has been contacted by a search or contingency firm, you will feel as if the recruiter or search professional does not have your best interests at heart. It will seem as if they only pay attention to you when they think you might be fit for a specific opening. And you will be absolutely right! The sooner you realize and accept this fact, the less frustrated you will be when dealing with contingency and search firms.

Go ahead and work with search or contingency firms, but do not rely solely on them to find your next job for you. In most cases, they will only be able to place you if you are looking for exactly the same type of position in the industry you work in now. *Rarely is a search firm paid a fee for placing a candidate who is making a career change.* Still, it's smart to develop long-standing relationships with search or contingency professionals, even if they can't place you. Refer candidates to them and always return their calls when they leave a message asking whom you might know for a search they are working on. A search or contingency professional is a good person to develop a networking relationship with over time. Just remember, they are salespeople whose compensation is contingent upon placing individuals with specific skills in specific jobs.

Interviewing

It is highly unusual to find a new job without going on a face-to-face interview, and these days, it's also common to meet and talk to a large number of people in an organization during the hiring process. If you are not capable of making an impressive presentation to the people with whom you are interviewing, you will not receive a job offer.

"Performing" well in interviews means several things: your physical image must be appealing to the interviewer; your verbal presentation must be interesting and focused on what you can bring to and do for the interviewer and his or her company; and you must demonstrate that you will "fit" well within the organization.

Interviewing, while stressful for many people, is a learned skill. Being prepared to talk about yourself and your past accomplishments succinctly and in a compelling manner is very important. If you've gone through some assessment and written a quality résumé, then you already are familiar with all of this information. Since you probably don't go on interviews every day, it is difficult to practice, but before going on a significant interview, ask friends, family, or a career counselor to role-play with you. Yet, oddly enough, most people don't do this. Preparing a list of questions for the interviewer and asking the same ones of everyone you meet at the company is another good idea. You can write down their answers, compare them later, and use the information to write customized thank-you notes. Some questions you might want to ask are:

- What do you think an average day in this position would be like?
- What would be your expectations of me in my first three months? Six months? A year?
- What are the biggest problems or challenges you are facing in this department or division?
- What reporting relationships would I have in this job?
- What kinds of people succeed here?
- What were the strengths of the person who was in this job previously?
- How would you describe the corporate culture here?

Remember that many people aren't necessarily very skilled at interviewing candidates. Therefore, as the interviewee, it is your responsibility to keep the conversation on track so that:

1. You can communicate everything you need to the interviewer before the interview ends.
2. You will get the information you need in order to move forward in the process.

Follow-up

Writing thank-you notes is a very important method of follow-up for both networking meetings and actual interviews. Whether your thanks are word-processed, handwritten, or in an e-mail isn't really the issue. Just do it! It adds to the positive impression the interviewer has of you. It also is an additional opportunity to sell yourself and to address any concerns on the interviewer's part that may have come up during the interview. Joanne, the vice president of human resources at an international trading company, observed that, sadly, only 10 percent of the applicants she interviews for nonexempt jobs and 50 percent of the applicants she interviews for exempt or managerial positions send thank-you notes. Marj, a director of human resources at a large utility, stated, "I think thank-you letters are becoming rarer and rarer, regardless of the job levels." This is too bad since, as she explains, these notes are another tool an applicant has: "They are a good way for a candidate to remind the interviewer of his or her name, reiterate interest in the position, and do a little sales pitch, too."

Everyone has had some experience looking for a job. Regardless of what this has been, there are several false beliefs about looking for a job that perpetually circulate and people seem to accept. This next section addresses the most prevalent myths and the truth about them.

Job Search Myths

Myths that people believe about looking for a job are many and persistent. The most common ones are:

Myth #1: A résumé should only be one page.

Absolutely not! The normal length of a résumé is two to three pages (at most). It is fine to have addendum pages such as a list of references or published articles.

Myth #2: If you go on an interview through a contingency or search firm, you cannot speak directly to the person who interviewed you after the interview.

The person who interviewed you is either a decision-maker or an influencer in the hiring process. Ask him during the interview if he minds if you contact him with any questions you may have later. If he says no, be skeptical about his interest or style. After all, you are the person who was on the interview, not the recruiting professional who set up your interview.

Myth #3: If eight people at a company interviewed you, you need only send a thank-you note to the person you'd report to if you got the job.

Those other seven people took their valuable time to interview you. Of course, you should send each one a thank-you note!

Myth #4: You shouldn't take notes during an interview.

Why not? Nobody has a photographic memory while talking, listening, and processing information. Simply ask the interviewer politely if she minds if you take some notes. Obviously, you should use abbreviations or keywords so that you're not concentrating too hard on taking notes and not focusing enough on the conversation.

Myth #5: There is no point in conducting a job search during the summer or in December because companies aren't hiring then.

This is absolutely ridiculous. In fact, during the summer, businesspeople are more casual and "laid back" in their attitudes and approaches. They don't tend to be as immersed in stressful projects. What a great time to approach people! In December, companies may be focused on bringing someone on board before the new calendar or fiscal year. People are in a much more celebratory mood during this time of year and December offers lots of opportunities for networking.

Myth #6: The most qualified candidate has the best shot at getting a job offer.

Obviously, for most positions, a company needs someone with specific skills and experience. It is also true that many companies still lean toward someone who has worked in the same industry. It is more likely that the individual who *fits* into the company culture is the one who will get the offer. This means that as a candidate, you are accountable for finding out and understanding what the culture is—the values that shape the company, the way people communicate, and the kinds of people who are respected within the organization. You will not find this kind of information on a Web site or in an annual report. You will find it from talking to people—the company's employees, vendors, and ex-employees.

Myth #7: Only certain components of a job offer are negotiable.

The two best times to negotiate with a company are when they ask you to join them, and when they ask you to leave. Anything can be negotiated if you are very clear about what you need and want, and can state the reasons why. You stand the best chance of getting your needs met if you put yourself in the company's shoes during the negotiation. Not only can compensation be negotiated, but also the work itself, the way you will do the work, whom you will report to, and every other aspect of the job.

Looking for a new job requires many skills, and the more you network, interview, and negotiate, the easier the process becomes. Above all, trust your instincts during your job search. As with any relationship, there are compromises that you may have to make. However, there is absolutely no reason why you shouldn't be able to find the right job—a job that fits your personality and fulfills your needs.

Afterword

A Conference Board survey in late 2000 showed that less than 51 percent of Americans were happy with their jobs, down from 59 percent in 1995. The Career Education Corporation, which runs thirty postsecondary schools, published a survey in 2000 that showed that half the employed adults in the United States would consider changing careers, and that nearly 25 percent planned on doing so within the next year. Only 3 percent said that they were satisfied in their current jobs. In 2001, *career-intelligence.com,* a career Web site for women, conducted a survey of its readers about career satisfaction. More than 50 percent said they were ready for a career change. According to a CareerBuilder.com survey, nearly four out of ten U.S. workers were seeking new job opportunities in 2001.

These statistics point to a pervasive dissatisfaction in the workplace today. On the other hand, it is now both accepted and expected that if you are unhappy, bored, or unfulfilled in your work, you *can* and *should* change what you are doing. In February 2001, *Working Woman* magazine ran an article by Lisa Belkin entitled "Reinvent Yourself," which proclaimed, "There is a revolution afoot in the workplace, and at its core is the simple fact that a remarkable number of us are not just willing but itching to get out there and reinvent ourselves. Bold career moves have become a virtual badge of courage."

Work is no longer just about completing tasks to make money for a company and its shareholders. Instead, it is about creating and maintaining a more equitable relationship between employee and employer or business owner and client. It is also about you as an individual needing and wanting choices, meaning, rewards, motivation, and success in your work. The path is different for each of us. If you are feeling dissatisfied or disillusioned with your current job, then your mission is not only to admit that you are dissatisfied, but to commit to creating a vision for the kind of work that will bring you satisfaction, to design a plan for implementing your vision. You can begin the journey of finding gratifying work right now!

There are thousands upon thousands of people who have successfully changed their work to reflect their needs and preferences. Here are a few stories of people who have done so and are happy.

Rita is a self-employed media consultant. At forty-six, she has taken what she's learned in the six careers she's already had (recruiting, the restaurant business, social services counseling, real estate sales, corporate relocation, and advertising sales) and created interesting new work for herself. "I've always wanted to do work that matters to me. I need to be passionate about what I do and I want to excel at it. Recently, I stepped off the cliff of the more secure corporate environment and have been successful in establishing myself as an independent consultant *and* I have enough work to be financially secure."

Greg, fifty-two, was a lawyer for twenty years. "I had to give in to the creative parts of me that I had not been pursuing during that career," he says. So he decided to stop practicing law and become a photographer. He now reports, "My job gives me the opportunity to make things with my hands, which is a kind of creativity that is most important to me."

At thirty-six, Jon was downsized from his job as a corporate human resources executive. He intentionally took over a year off from working to "figure out what I wanted to do." Why? While he was successful in his job, he did not find it fulfilling. "I thought I was sophisticated when I started my introspective journey and found it more difficult than I expected. There's no language and no definite path to searching for the right work. I do feel that there is a path that is different for everyone." While Jon knows he needs to find challenging and engaging work, at the same time he wants to live a more holistic life, something he believes is difficult to do while one is caught up in the corporate whirlwind.

During his hiatus, Jon went through an extensive rediscovery process using the Crystal-Barkley method (*The Crystal-Barkley Guide to Taking Charge of Your Career,* by Nella Barkley and Eric Sandburg), which included writing a thirty-page story of his life. What did he decide to do? He thinks he'll end up in human resources again, but with an employer who believes strongly in human capital and isn't simply focused on making a profit. Now that he has refreshed his understanding of himself and what's important to him, Jon feels better equipped to find fulfillment—as opposed to just "success"—in his work.

While it's important to experience tangible success in your work—that is, achieving the business goals that you and your employer have set—once you have done this, the meaning can fade quickly. Teri, thirty-five, sells a music service. She has ranked as the number-one salesperson in her company for six years. Teri is Bored and Plateaued. "Who cares if I make the top of the list again?" she says. "It just does not mean anything to me anymore." Teri is planning a start-up venture, manufacturing and selling acrylic frames for parents' ultrasound pictures of their babies in utero. "This is a project from my heart. So I love it," says Teri. "Ultraframes fuel my creative side. This will be a huge challenge—I cannot wait."

Michael practiced law his entire career. At sixty, he bought a wine store franchise, opening a brand-new location for the franchisor. In his first six months, Michael's sales ranked in the top percentage of all the company's franchises in the United States. More important, Michael is "extremely satisfied and gratified to be working for myself and deciding on my own destiny and future." Michael had been in the Yearning to Be on Your Own situation for a long time because "I was tired and fed up working for incompetent managers who were where they were because of who they knew and not what they knew. I just wanted to be the 'captain of my own ship.'"

Jack retired at sixty-three from a thirty-year career in the chemical industry. At sixty-nine, he works full-time as a senior consultant for a research company that supports his former industry. He holds three significant leadership roles for volunteer organizations as well. When Jack isn't working sixty hours a week, he flies a plane, sails, kayaks, and collects cameras. When Jack was asked how long he thought he'd keep working, he replied, "Probably another ten years."

In her book *What Do You Want to Be When You Grow Up?* psychologist Dorothy Cantor makes an important point that "previously defined visions can fade in importance over time. Life keeps happening, and transitions are part of it." The point of this book is to help you to realize that being satisfied, happy, fulfilled, or exhilarated with your work is up to you . . . and you alone.

Caroline, at forty, owns a contracting/consulting company. She works with engineering firms as a program manager for a technical research project on rail transportation crashworthiness and safety. Both her bachelor's and master's degrees are in engineering, but when she actually worked as an engineer, she was never truly satisfied. Now she uses her engineering background in a nonengineering role and finds her work very meaningful. With two children, Caroline needs to work to supplement her husband's income, yet she is able to have some downtime between consulting projects.

Caroline created her own work by taking self-assessment tests, which helped her to define her strengths, and interests. Then she took action by designing work that would enable her to bring in income and spend time with her young children.

When Caroline responded to the question "Are you satisfied with your current job?," her answer was, "I absolutely LOVE what I do. I enjoy managing and scheduling my own time; I enjoy the extreme diversity of my jobs. I like being able to do something else during the downtimes of one contract and having an impact on two separate projects, instead of whittling my time away on one job and filling in the down times with unnecessary busy work."

It's time to make yourself happy in your work. Start your journey today. As Jon, the human resources executive, said earlier, it's not necessarily easy to find your path toward finding satisfying work. This is why more people choose *not* to do anything about alleviating their unhappiness or dissatisfaction. Don't let yourself be one of them. Instead, close your eyes and allow yourself to imagine what it would feel like to be happy and excited and fulfilled in your work. Finding work that is satisfying, gratifying, and fulfilling will change your life!

Resources

Chapter 1: Why Do You Want or Need to Change Your Work?

Age Works, by Beverly Goldberg. The Free Press, 2000. A guide for corporations and the business community that shows ways to meet the needs of older workers. This book is filled with statistics and creative approaches to looking at retirement, recruitment, and employee retention.

Don't Stop the Career Clock, by Helen Harkness. Davies-Black Publishing, 1999. Advocates the need to stop designing and living our lives on the basis of chronological time, focusing instead on functional age. It provides action steps and exercises for doing this.

Generations at Work, by Ron Zemke, Claire Raines, and Bob Filipczak. AMACOM, 2000. An overview of four generational groups and what each wants and needs, including several case studies that describe company cultures that embrace generational differences, as well as tips and techniques offered in the form of questions.

The Working Life, by Joanne B. Ciulla. Times Books, 2000. An overview of the history, mythology, pop culture, and management theory of work; it presents a critical look at how work impacts our lives.

Chapter 2: What Is Your Work Situation?

Clicking: 16 Trends to Future Fit Your Life, Your Work, and Your Business, by Faith Popcorn and Lys Marigold. Harper Audio, 1996. Moving forward from the best-selling *Popcorn Report,* the authors identify and chart the sixteen trends they consider critical to making the right choices in business and in life.

Dare to Change Your Job and Your Life, by Carole Kanchier, Ph.D. Jist Works, 2000. Kanchier gives an overview of how to change your work and your life using the "Quester," her description of a "creative risk taker." The content is based upon what she learned from thirty thousand interviews with individuals.

The Future of Success, by Robert B. Reich. Alfred A. Knopf, 2001. Reich considers the likely consequences of rapid equalization of access to information and "acquisitive individualism" in an economy driven by unrelenting competition. The book will help you understand your choices as you define "success" in your career.

The Future of Work: The Promise of the New Digital Work Society, by Charles E. Grantham. McGraw-Hill Professional Publishing, 1999. Grantham paints a compelling portrait of how the new workplace—already taking shape—is creating a new framework for the way people think about and act at work, whether at home, in a satellite office, or at corporate headquarters.

Futurework: Trends and Challenges for Work in the 21st Century, by United States Department of Labor. Jist Works, 2000. This book outlines workplace trends in the areas of labor and industrial relations, career choice and guidance, job opportunities, and planning and forecasting.

Some Interesting Web Sites:

Fast Company magazine. *www.fastcompany.com.* A site that is designed to guide you through various career cycles, including building your business, leading your team, going solo, reinventing yourself, launching your career, and being a change

agent. It provides customized stories, interactive tools, and expert opinions, all focused on your career in the "new economy."
Institute for the Study of Distributed Work. *www.isdw.com.* The site's mission is "to increase society's knowledge and understanding of distributed work so that industry, community and individual needs can be met simultaneously."

Two Good Overview Articles:

"21st-Century Workplace Trends," report by Challenger, Gray & Christmas (outplacement consulting firm), 2000. *www.ipma-hr.org/hrhead/trends.html.*

"21st-Century Workplace Trends and Their Implications," by Joseph Boyett (principal of Boyett & Associates), 2000. *www.jboyett.com/trends.htm.*

Chapter 3: Values, Attitudes, and Change Readiness, and Chapter 4: Personality Preferences, Interests, and Favorite Skills

Do What You Are: Discover the Perfect Career for You Through the Secrets of Personality Type, by Paul Tieger and Barbara Barron-Tieger. 3rd ed. Little, Brown & Company, 2001. Based on the Myers Briggs Type Indicator, this book introduces personality types and aligns them with suggested careers. Many occupations are listed that are popular with specific personality types, including careers in biotech, new media, e-commerce, and telecommunications.

Taking Charge of Your Career, by Nella Barkley and Eric Sandburg. Workman Publishing, 1995. Based upon the Crystal-Barkley career-planning system, this book is a comprehensive guide that takes readers from finding out what they want to do to landing a job they want.

Tests and Examinations: Measuring Abilities and Performance, by Lewis R. Aiken. John Wiley & Sons, 1998. A book/computer disk package that reviews the conceptual foundations of psychological testing and provides guidelines and computer programs for planning, administering, and scoring tests in educational, clinical, business, and government settings.

Test Your Own Job Aptitude, by Jim Barrett and Geoff Williams. Penguin Books, 1990. This book is filled with tests and questionnaires focused on assessing abilities, personality, and motivation. It is geared toward entry-level employees or people in their first career.

Some Useful Web Sites:

CareerPerfect.com. *www.careerperfect.com.* A comprehensive career-planning site, with on-line career-planning tools and tests; advice for and samples of résumés, e-résumés, and cover letters; job search advice and resources; interview advice and tools; and articles on such topics as employment trends and coping with unemployment.

CareerPlanner.com. *www.careerplanner.com.* This site provides information on the career-planning process, a reading list in career planning, and a career-planning test.

Careers By Design. *www.careers-by-design.com.* This site offers affordable, statistically reliable, and valid assessments for individual career planning, determining personality type, and corporate team development (Strong Interest Inventory, MBTI, FIRO-B, 16PF).

Compass Point. *www.compasspointonline.com./careerassess.html.* A site that provides on-line career assessments for individuals and hiring and training assessment tools for businesses.

ERICAE.NET. *ericae.net* A clearinghouse for assessment, evaluation, and research information.

JobBankUSA.com. *www.jobbankusa.com.* In addition to being a job search clearinghouse, the site offers a free career analysis, including the Motivational Appraisal of Personal Potential (MAPP) to discover natural motivations, interests, and talents for work.

Chapter 5: Where's the Meaning?

The Artist's Way, by Julia Cameron. Jeremy P. Tarcher/Putnam, 1992. A twelve-week program for recovering creativity using journaling as a method for doing so. It was written for artists and people in creative occupations, but it is a useful guide for nonartists as well.

Careers for Doers and Dreamers: A Guide to Management Careers in the Non Profit Sector, by Lilly Cohen and Dennis R. Young. The Foundation Center, 1989. The authors profile nonprofit executives and managers, fund-raisers and foundation officials, describing their job responsibilities and the career paths that led them to their positions. They also discuss employment and compensation packages in the nonprofit world and offer advice on how to conduct a job search.

Do What You Love, the Money Will Follow: Discovering Your Right Livelihood, by Marsha Sinetar. DTP, 1989. Although an older book, it still helps you discover how to tune into your inner world and your unique talents, evaluate and build your self-esteem, banish your outmoded network of "shoulds," deal with resistance, and liberate yourself from an unfulfilling job.

From Making a Profit to Making a Difference—How to Launch Your New Career in Non Profits, by Richard King. Planning Communications, 2000. This step-by-step guide for making the transition from the business world to starting a career in the nonprofit world includes an assessment that will help you to identify which nonprofit you'll flourish at, and directories of executive recruiters and resources.

Good Works: A Guide to Careers in Social Change, by Donna Clovin and Ralph Nader. 5th ed. Barricade Books, 1994. This is a giant directory of information on more than one thousand social change organizations. It also profiles individuals who are building new careers around their social concerns.

The Harvard Business School Guide to Careers in the Non Profit Sector, by Stephanie Lowell. Harvard Business School Press, 2000. A resource guide that is directed toward M.B.A.s who are interested in entering the nonprofit sector as board members, full-time employees, or volunteers. It covers careers in the arts and culture, community economic development, education, environment, foundations, government, health care, international aid, social services, and economic development.

Inner Excellence at Work: The Path to Meaning, Spirit, and Success, by Carol Orsborn. AMACOM, 1999. Using the seven principles found in this guide, you can learn to work less but achieve more; tap into new sources of inspiration, creativity, and vitality; change your beliefs about business and life and the way you manage your career; and find lasting happiness and success in chaotic, unstable times.

Making a Living While Making a Difference, by Melissa Everett. 2nd ed. New Society Publishers, 1999. Unlike traditional career guides that focus on defining skill areas, this one focuses on personal, social, and environmental values as the driving force for career decisions. It includes self-assessments, exercises, and visualizations that help you define your personal area of commitment.

The Passion Plan, by Richard Chang. Jossey-Bass Publishers, 2000. A guide that describes a seven-step process for discovering and understanding what passion is for you and using it to build your life.

The Power of Purpose: Creating Meaning in Your Life and Work, by Richard Leider. Berrett-Koehler Publishers, 1997. A down-to-earth guide for people who want to combine their "own unique gifts" with "the needs of the world" to carve out a vocational niche that's both individualized and highly rewarding. It includes a helpful guide to using the material in a reading group.

Some Nonprofit Organizations:

American Red Cross. This organization helps keep people safe every day as well as in emergencies. 800-662-2531.

America's Promise—The Alliance for Youth, led by Colin Powell. The organization's focus is on improving the lives of America's youth through mentoring and other support efforts. 703-684-4500.

America's Second Harvest. This is the nation's largest domestic hunger relief organization. 800-771-2303.

Global Volunteers. This is a private, international tax-exempt organization in special consultative status with the United Nations. 800-487-1074.

Habitat for Humanity. This organization works in partnership with people in need of building and renovating decent, affordable housing. 800-442-5914.

Literacy Volunteers of America. This organization recruits and trains volunteers to tutor basic literary understanding of English to people who speak other languages. 877-435-7582.

Chapter 6: Been There, Done That, but Still Need to Earn

The Nine Steps to Financial Freedom, by Suze Orman. Crown Publishers, 1997. This is a book that describes the nine steps one must take to realize financial freedom. Orman covers your attitudes about money, managing money, and understanding and respecting money.

Chapter 7: Bruised and Gun-shy

Are You a Corporate Refugee?, by Ruth Luban. Penguin Books, 2000. This guide outlines the five steps someone who has been displaced by the workplace can take to heal and recover from their experience.

The New Corporate Cultures: Revitalizing the Workplace After Downsizing, Mergers, and Reengineering, by Terrence E. Deal and Allan A. Kennedy. Perseus Books, 1999. The authors provide an assessment of the difficulties that face corporate cultures. A diagnostic of these problems is presented with alternative models suggested as solutions for achieving corporate renewal.

A Useful Web Site:

www.jobstresshelp.com. This site provides tips and statistics on how to deal with the stress that work can create. Responses to various surveys conducted on workplace stress are shown.

Chapter 8: Bored and Plateaued

The Pathfinder, by Nicholas Lore. Simon & Schuster: A Fireside Book, 1998. This comprehensive book guides you through the process of designing the career you want. It is filled with self-tests and diagnostic tools to help you to understand yourself and design work that will fit your personality, goals, needs, and values.

Chapter 9: Yearning to Be on Your Own

Being a "Free Agent"

Executive Temp, by Diane L. Thrailkill. Random House, 1999. This practical guide offers real world tips from already successful "career temps" for finding and maneuvering through temporary assignments.

Free Agent Nation, by Daniel H. Pink. Warner Books, 2001. Pink describes America's new economic icon: the "free agent" or self-employed independent worker. He shows who these free agents are—from marketing consultant to home-based entrepreneur to technology contractor—and explains why they've forged this new path, and how they are shaking up our political, educational, and family institutions.

Successful Freelancing: The Complete Guide to Establishing and Running Any Kind of Freelance Business, by Marian Faux. Rev. ed. St. Martin's Press, 1997. Faux provides writers, consultants, artists, and all other types of freelancers with the essential information they need to set up and run a profitable, successful business. Special emphasis is placed on the concerns of women running their own businesses, as well as parents and couples working from home.

"The Word Is Out: Becoming a Free Agent Is a Hot Career Path," by Randall S. Hansen, is an extremely helpful article published at QuintCareers.com, 2001. *www.quintcareers.com/ becoming_a_ free_agent.html.*

A Useful Web Site:

FreeAgent.com. *www.freeagent.com.* This site acts as a clearinghouse for consultants and employers. It also provides many business services for free agents (e-mail, personal 800 number, secretarial services) and a variety of advice and resources.

Working as a Solo Practitioner

The Business of Consulting: The Basics and Beyond, by Elaine Biech. Pfeiffer & Co., 1998. Biech considers all phases of a typical consulting business, from start-up and attracting new business to subcontracting and balancing personal and professional responsibilities. It includes a disk of documents and worksheets.

The Consultant's Toolkit: High-Impact Questionnaires, Activities and How-to Guides for Diagnosing and Solving Client Problems, Melvin L. Silberman, ed. McGraw-Hill, 2000. A collection of field-tested tools, customizable questionnaires, and techniques for working with clients, this book provides crucial problem-solving help in such areas as managing and leading change, organizational initiatives, assessing team and organizational functioning, improving relationships between departments and business units, and creative problem-solving techniques.

Flawless Consulting: A Guide to Getting Your Expertise Used, by Peter Block. 2nd ed. Jossey-Bass, 1999. The consultant's "bible" for more than fifteen years, this book describes and demonstrates ways of behaving with clients. It includes illustrative examples, case studies, exercises, and commentary on pitfalls.

Million Dollar Consulting, by Alan Weiss. 2nd ed. McGraw Hill, 1997. Written for the owner of a small consulting practice, this book offers pithy and hard-hitting yet commonsense advice about client contracts, setting fees based on value not time, and common mistakes that consultants make with pricing, ethics, joint ventures, and more.

Soloing, by Harriet Rubin. Harper Business, 1999. This book is an autobiographical account of the author's journey toward becoming a soloist.

Buying a Franchise

Franchise Bible: How to Buy a Franchise or Franchise Your Own, by Erwin J. Keup. PSI Successful Business Library, 2000. This book is a practical and complete guide on every aspect of buying or starting a franchise. It contains information about how to determine whether you would be a suitable franchisee or franchisor, the advantages and disadvantages of the franchise marketing system, the terms and conditions of a franchise agreement, and checklists and forms to help you organize the process.

Franchise Organization, by Jeffrey L. Bradach. Harvard Business School Press, 1998. This book surveys the key factors that shape a franchise business's success. Major restaurant chains are used as examples of the components needed to create and run a thriving franchise enterprise.

A Useful Web Site:

www.franchise.com. This site provides information on buying domestic and international franchises, finding real estate, and financing your franchise.

Buying a Business

The following are two good overview articles on buying a business:

"Basics of Buying a Business," Small Business Exchange of American Express Small Business Services. 2000. *http://home3. americanexpress.com/smallbusiness/resources/starting/buybiz.shtml.*

"Buying a Business," Entrepreneurs at About.com. 2000. *www. entrepreneurs.about.com.*

A Useful Web Site:

www.bizbuysell.com. This site lists thousands of established businesses for sale, forms, checklists, and interactive worksheets and recommendations of articles, books, and Web sites to help you buy a business.

Selling How-tos

The New Strategic Selling: The Unique Sales System Proven Successful by the World's Best Companies, by Stephen E. Heiman et al. Warner Books, 1998. Heiman provides a straightforward, structured, and repeatable sales system that replaces uncertainty with knowledge about oneself and the customer, and shows a practical path to creating value-based, long-lasting, and satisfying customer relationships.

Selling for People Who Hate to Sell, by Brigid McGrath Massie. Prima Publishing, 1996. This is a guide for nonsalespeople, with basics on topics from making a first impression to follow-through.

Solution Selling: Creating Buyers in Difficult Selling Markets, by Michael T. Bosworth. McGraw-Hill, 1995. Bosworth teaches new salespeople critical sales skills and allows experienced salespeople to fine-tune their skills. He uses a comprehensive methodology for emphasizing business issues rather than product.

Spin Selling, by Neil Rackham. McGraw-Hill, 1988. This book is a classic work that continues to be relevant. Rackham divides the sale into four phases: The Preliminaries, Investigating, Demonstrating Capability, and Obtaining Commitment, and emphasizes asking questions according to the SPIN model (Situation, Problem, Implication, Need-Payoff).

Visionary Selling: How to Get to Top Executives, and How to Sell Them When You're There, by Barbara Geraghty et al. Simon & Schuster, 1998. Geraghty describes how to become a business ally of your customers, turn gatekeepers into allies, use the Internet for research, approach executives through e-mail, and craft a pertinent and provocative presentation.

Starting Your Own Business

Anatomy of a Business Plan: A Step-by-Step Guide to Starting Smart, Building the Business, and Securing Your Company's Future, by Linda Pinson and Jerry Jinnett. 4th ed. Dearborn Trade, 1999. Pinson and Jinnett give a step-by-step process for developing a polished, professional, and results-oriented plan. The book includes the latest marketing strategies that incorporate the Web, an explanation of financial assumptions, and a list of useful resources.

Keeping the Books: Basic Recordkeeping and Accounting for the Successful Small Business, by Linda Pinson. 5th ed. Dearborn Trade, 2001. This is a durable guide that helps you prepare and analyze financial statements to stay in touch with the heart of your business, set up bookkeeping systems to keep track of financial details, maintain the required IRS records necessary to stay out of trouble, and plan for required taxes due.

Low Risk, High Reward: Starting and Growing Your Business with Minimal Risk, by Bob Reiss and Jeffrey L. Cruikshank. The Free Press, 2000. Reiss and Cruikshank address practical methods for spotting, managing, and reducing risks in virtually every facet of business, from developing initial concepts and financing production to securing orders and preparing for the future.

Small Time Operator: How to Start Your Own Business, Keep Your Books, Pay Your Taxes, and Stay Out of Trouble, by Bernard B. Kamoroff. 25th ed. Bell Springs Publishers, 2000. This "bible" of the industry presents all the nuts and bolts of building a business, from obtaining initial permits and licenses to locating financing, finding the right business location, developing a bookkeeping system, and hiring employees.

Successful Business Planning in 30 Days: A Step-by-Step Guide for Writing a Business Plan and Starting Your Own Business, by Peter J. Patsula. Patsula Media, 2000. This book has all the basics for starting your own business, with real-life examples and suggestions in a usable and practical workbook format. It provides the charts, wooksheets, and graphs needed to make decisions.

Thinking Like an Entrepreneur: How to Make Intelligent Business Decisions That Will Lead to Success in Building & Growing Your Own Company, by Peter I. Hupalo. Hupalo, Ltd., 1999. Hupalo covers such topics as risk assessment, basic accounting, managing resources, writing a business plan, and calculating profits, but the emphasis of the book is how to think like an entrepreneur.

What No One Ever Tells You About Starting Your Own Business: Real-Life Start-up Advice from 101 Successful Entrepreneurs, by Jan Norman. Upstart Publishing Co., 1999. Using more than one hundred interviews with seasoned entrepreneurs, Norman guides you through every stage of business start-up, from planning to marketing, and provides eye-opening lessons from successful business owners who've learned the hard way.

Some Useful Web Sites:

Bplans.com. *www.bplans.com.* In addition to advice on topics ranging from starting a business to helpful business software to reading lists for effective start-ups, this site includes a variety of sample business plans you can search that match your business.

Inc. magazine. *www.Inc.com.* This site contains information about how to plan and start a small business and advice for small

business owners about topics like technology, hiring and motivating employees, marketing, and customer service.

Success magazine. *www.Successmagazine.com.* This is a site that contains trends, tips, and ideas for entrepreneurs, as well as profiles
of successful entrepreneurs.

U.S. Small Business Administration. *www.sba.gov.* A vast site
with information on starting a business, financing, business opportunities, disaster assistance, local offices, SCORE resources
in your area, and more.

Chapter 10: One Toe in the Retirement Pool

*Prime Time: How Baby-Boomers Will Revolutionize Retirement and Trans-
form America,* by Marc Freedman. Public Affairs Press, 2000.
Freedman explores the idea that baby boomers will turn their
golden years into an intense time of social activism, volun-
teerism, and lifelong learning—if government and business can
create programs that capitalize on their love of learning and community service, as well as wipe out ageism and other barriers.

*Retire Early and Live the Life You Want Now: A 10-Step Plan for Rein-
venting Your Retirement,* by John F. Wasik. Henry Holt, 2000. Not
just a guide on spending, structuring income, and selecting the
best investment strategies, this book also includes questionnaires and personal inventories designed to elicit, distill, and
refine the values and pursuits important to you. It also includes
sections listing additional references and resources, many available on-line.

Retirement on a Shoestring, by John Howells. The Globe Pequot
Press, 2000. Howells provides up-to-date information on topics like quality housing, the best affordable retirement locations, real estate taxes, and retiring in foreign countries.

Smart Guide to Planning for Retirement, by Mike Robbins. John
Wiley & Sons, 1999. This is a comprehensive guide about all of
the financial aspects of planning for retirement, including calculating how much someone needs to retire, Social Security,
employer-sponsored retirement plans, and investments. Robbins also dedicates a chapter to situations that can threaten re-

tirement, such as ill parents, divorce, the death of a spouse, and stock market meltdowns.

The Wall Street Journal Guide to Planning Your Financial Future: The Easy-to-Read Guide to Planning for Retirement, by Alan M. Siegel, Virginia B. Morris, and Kenneth M. Morris. Rev. ed. Simon & Schuster: Fireside Press, 1998. The authors provide clear guidelines for the decisions one has to make to enjoy a comfortable retirement, covering such topics as the advantages of salary reduction plans, the difference between Roth and traditional IRAs, and the benefits of effective tax planning.

You're Fifty—Now What? Investing for the Second Half of Your Life, by Charles R. Schwab. Crown Publishers, 2000. Schwab helps you take stock of everything you've accumulated, determine how much it costs you to live now, estimate what it will take to maintain that lifestyle into the future, and invest properly to fund your plan.

Your Next Fifty Years: A Completely New Way to Look at How, When, and If You Should Retire, by Ginita Wall and Victoria Collins. Henry Holt, 1997. The authors combine psychology and financial planning to explore practical alternatives to traditional retirement, such as sabbaticals, flextime, and temporary or part-time retirement. They use worksheets, tables, and "Smart Tips" to offer information on investment choices, insurance and estate planning, and specific retirement issues faced by women.

Some Useful Web Sites:

AARP. *www.aarp.org.* From America's leading organization for people age fifty and older, this site provides information and education about health and wellness, leisure and fun, legislative issues, life transitions, money, work, volunteering, and computers and technology.

Money.com. *money.com/money/depts/retirement.* In addition to covering many retirement topics like choosing appropriate investment vehicles, setting up family trusts, and understanding the roles of pensions, 401(k)s, IRAs, and the like, this site offers retirement savings calculators, cost of living calculators, and a tool for finding the best place to retire.

Quicken.com. *quicken.com/retirement.* This site contains general financial information and a good selection of pages on retirement basics like 401(k)s, pension plans, IRAs, Social Security, and a retirement planner as well as special topics like taking care of aging parents and planning for inflation. It also offers software for retirement planning.

Social Security Retirement Planner. *www.ssa.gov/retire.* This government site provides information on eligibility factors affecting retirement benefits, options available as you near retirement, and several benefit calculators using different retirement scenarios.

www.2young2retire.com. This is the site that is geared toward people who are forty-five and older and are interested in new careers, businesses, volunteer work, and adventures. It features people who have made radical lifestyle and career changes as well as links to other sites on careers, learning, volunteering, and wellness.

Chapter 11: The Ten Keys to Success

Attitude Is Everything: 10 Life-Changing Steps to Turning Attitude into Action, by Keith Harrell. Cliff Street Books, 2000. This book teaches ten steps for an "attitude tune-up" that turns "attitude into action."

Emotional Intelligence, by Daniel Goleman. Bantam Books, 1995. A popular research-based book that makes the case for emotional intelligence being the strongest indicator of human success. Emotional intelligence is defined in terms of self-awareness, altruism, personal motivation, empathy, and the ability to love and be loved.

Learned Optimism: How to Change Your Mind and Your Life, by Martin Seligman, Ph.D. Pocket Books, 1998. This groundbreaking classic provides a psychological discussion of pessimism, optimism, learned helplessness, and depression and how these affect success, health, and quality of life. The book teaches how to turn pessimism into optimism with worksheet pages.

Chapter 12: Job Search—the Nuts and Bolts

Job Search How-tos

The Accelerated Job Search, by Wayne D. Ford. The Management Advantage, 1999. This book lays out a sequential approach to getting organized, setting up an effective strategy, and following proven methods in achieving success in finding the job you want.

Ask the Headhunter: Reinventing the Interview to Win the Job, by Nicholas Corcodilos. Plume Books, 1997. A guide to "the new interview," a unique and aggressive method for job hunters to prepare for interviews and effectively showcase their expertise. Easy to read, with boxed "sentences to remember" and worksheets.

The Complete Job-Search Handbook: Everything You Need to Know to Get the Job You Really Want, by Howard E. Figler. 3rd ed. Owl Books, 1999. A durable guide, updated to include thirty lifetime job-hunting skills and twenty potential pitfalls to avoid, that helps you determine what your true work and life values are, pinpoint the job skills you already possess, be your best in job interviews, and use a career counselor's advice to troubleshoot potential problems.

Games Companies Play: The Job Hunter's Guide to Playing Smart and Winning Big in the High-Stakes Hiring Game, by Pierre Mornell and Kit Hinrichs. Ten Speed Press, 2000. Mornell, the author of *Hiring Smart* (1998), applies his inside corporate intelligence to the job seeker's perspective. The book includes strategies for job hunting and also describes the strengths and weaknesses of sixteen different personality types.

101 Great Answers to Toughest Interview Questions, by Ronald W. Fry. 4th ed. Career Press, 1000. This book outlines an organized process for preparing for job interviews, beginning with thoughtful self-examination to determine how your strengths, interests, and background fit with the interviewing company. Audiocassette version lets you practice out loud in role-playing examples.

110 Best Job Search Sites on the Internet, by Katherine K. Yonge. Linx Education Publishers, 1998. This book focuses on the top Internet sites for locating companies you want to work for, posting résumés, learning job interviewing skills, and obtaining career-planning information.

60 Seconds and You're Hired, by Robin Ryan. Penguin Books, 2000. Ryan provides concise advice and easy techniques for mastering an interview.

What Color Is Your Parachute? A Practical Manual for Job-Hunters and Career-Changers, by Richard N. Bolles. Ten Speed Press, 2001. First published in 1970 and updated frequently, this book remains a classic in the field.

Some Useful Web Sites:

CareerJournal from the *Wall Street Journal. www.careerjournal.com.* This site provides a résumé database; lets you create a job search "agent" that searches for jobs meeting your criteria and reports results to you via e-mail; and provides salary and hiring information, job-hunting advice, tips on managing your career, and information on executive recruiters, as well as topical news stories.

HotJobs.com. *www.hotjobs.com.* One of the largest Internet job sites, with job postings in more than twenty-eight categories in the United States, Canada, and Australia. It also hosts on-line career expos, forums, and job fairs.

Job-Search-Engine. *www.job-search-engine.com/searchjob.* Not a job board, but an "infomediary" Web site that searches the top three hundred U.S. and Canadian job boards in parallel and in real time. Lets you specify a variety of job criteria and locations to search in.

Monster.com. *www.monster.com.* This is a "monster" site with more than three thousand pages of career advice, résumés, and salary information, as well as a vast job-posting database. Additional features include opportunities for senior executives, advice on relocating, and a database for free agents.

Résumé Writing

Asher's Bible of Executive Résumés and How to Write Them, by Donald Asher. Ten Speed Press, 1996. Résumés are not written the way they used to be, and this book explains how to do it right for today's world. Asher reviews techniques and styles and provides more than one hundred examples for many different types of backgrounds and job classes.

High-Impact Résumés and Letters: How to Communicate Your Qualifications to Employers, by Ronald L. Krannich and Caryl Krannich. 7th ed. Impact Publications, 1998. A best-seller that provides step-by-step guidance for developing each section of résumés and cover letters. It includes critical distribution, evaluation, and follow-up devices, as well as advice on conducting an effective job search.

Writing Your Resumé, by Simon Howard. Dorling Kindersley Publishers, 1999. One of DK's "Essential Managers" series, this book continues this publisher's trademark clarity of presentation. It walks you through the entire résumé-writing (or rewriting) process, and includes sample résumés, checklists, and flowcharts; it also provides tips on replying to job advertisements, canvassing employers, and using the Internet.

An Interesting Web Site:

Bakos Group. *www.800-370-jobs.com.* In addition to being "the world's largest résumé, career management, employment, and outplacement service," and providing the traditional job search capabilities, this site will give you a free critique of your résumé.

Networking

Dig Your Well Before You're Thirsty: The Only Networking Book You'll Ever Need, by Harvey Mackay. Doubleday, 1999. This book distills Mackay's years of wisdom *(Swim with the Sharks, Beware the Naked Man Who Offers You His Shirt)* on what kinds of networks exist, how to start and get the most from a network, the smart way to downsize your list, and what you can do if you're not good at small talk.

A Foot in the Door: Networking Your Way into the Hidden Job Market, by Katharine Hansen. Ten Speed Press, 2000. A no-nonsense guide to advancing your career by using the skills and strategies of networking.

Masters of Networking, by Ivan R. Misner and Don Morgan. Bard Press, 2000. The authors bring together the insights and examples of top networkers, telling you how they generate leads and referrals, build healthy relationships, and deliver value over the long term.

Power Networking: 59 Secrets for Personal and Professional Success, by Donna Fisher, Sandy Vilas, and Marilyn Hermance. 2nd ed. Bard Press, 2000. This book teaches you how to create personal and professional networks, with a self-assessment quiz to get started and several methods of eliminating the roadblocks to successful networking.

Power Networking: Using the Contacts You Don't Even Know You Have to Succeed in the Job You Want, by Marc Kramer. VGM Career Horizons, 1997. Kramer offers step-by-step instructions for identifying how many contacts you really have, how to make the most of these relationships, what organizations to join, and what to do at networking events.

Some Useful Web Sites:

MyJobSearch.com. *www.myjobsearch.com.* This site provides information on career planning, résumé writing, interviewing, employers, negotiating, and relocation. The pages on networking are especially good, covering associations, government leaders, colleges and universities, career fairs, a people finder, and a good reading list on the topic.

Quintessential Careers. *www.quintcareers.com.* In addition to access to traditional job search and career planning information, this site provides a collection of networking resources on the Internet, general networking organizations, professional organizations and associations, women's networking and professional organizations, a reading list, and an interviewing tutorial.

Search Firms

Headhunters Revealed! Career Secrets for Choosing and Using Professional Recruiters, by Darrell W. Gurney. Hunter Arts Publishing, 2000. Gurney demystifies what recruiters do, and shares witty and practical advice that helps you take advantage of the recruitment system to get the best job you can.

Job Seekers Guide to Executive Recruiters, by Christopher W. Hunt and Scott Scanlon. John Wiley & Sons, 1997. These authors provide in-depth listings for more than 5,200 executive search consultants, as well as expert advice on what to do before contacting recruiters, how to work with them to achieve the results you want, crafting effective résumés and cover letters, and preparing for interviews.

The Secrets of Executive Search: Professional Strategies for Managing Your Personal Job Search, by Robert M. Melancon. Melancon & Co., 2000. Inspired by the new workplace paradigm that says individuals must now manage their own careers, this book provides proven, real-world techniques for successful job search and career management.

Index

roadblocks and opportunities
in, 108–17
self-assessment for, 103–8
BT Novations, 123
burnout, 4
business, vision statement for,
170–71
business ownership, 13, 141
buying a preexisting business, 149, 159–64
twenty-six things to do when
starting a business, 175–
77
see also "Yearning to Be on
Your Own" situation
business plan, 171–75
company overview, 172
executive summary, 172–
73
financial plan, 174–75
management plan, 173–
74
marketing plan, 173
Business Week, 142

C

Cameron, Julia, 79–80
Cantor, Dorothy, 238
career, *see* work and career
CareerBuilder.com, 235
Career Education Corporation,
235
career-intelligence.com, 235
cash flow, in starting own business, 167–68
cause, contribution to, 65–66,
74–75

challenges and rewards, as type
of meaning, 65
Chang, Richard, 76
change readiness:
fear of the unknown, 223–24,
227
in self-assessments, 26, 38–40,
44, 107, 144
changing lifestyle:
concerns about, 76
as type of meaning, 65
charity organizations, 78
Cole, Neal, 191
company culture, 112–14, 233–
34
company overview, in business
plan, 172
Compass Point Consulting, 25–
26
Conference Board, 235
consultants, 149
contingency firms, 229–30
interviews and, 232–33
contingency workforce, 13
contributing/making a difference, 65, 74–75
Cooper, Glen, 159
corporate acquisitions and mergers, 4–5, 108
corporate refugees, 99, 102, 116
Corsearch, 173–74
creating/innovating, as type of
meaning, 66
creativity, insecurities about,
79–80
*Crystal-Barkley Guide to Taking
Charge of Your Career, The*
(Barkley and Sandburg), 237
curiosity, 199, 200–201

people, interest in, in self-
assessment, 52
perseverance, 199, 204–6
personality preferences, in self-
assessment, 41–46
personal life, balance between
work and, 7–8
Personnel Decisions International, 7
plateauing, 123
see also "Bored and Plateaued"
situation
*Plateauing Trap, The: How to
Avoid It in Your Career and in
Your Life* (Bardwick),
123
problem solving:
as type of meaning, 65
in unknown field of work,
75–76
professional commitment, in
self-assessments, 36, 37, 87,
106–7
promotions, 124

R

Raines, Claire, 5
realistic career goals, 93
realist personality, in self-
assessment, 44, 45
"Reinvent Yourself" (Belkin),
235–36
relationships:
in job search, 217–18
in self-assessments, 36, 37,
86, 105

researching career paths, 93–94
resources, entrepreneurship
and, 168–69
resources, guide to, 240–59
respect, 200, 215
résumé, 224–26
Internet, 225–26
length of, 232
retainer firms, 229–30
retirement:
age and, 179
financial aspects of, 180–81,
185–87, 194
reasons for considering, 180–
81
Social Security and, 8, 186–
87, 194
see also "One Toe in the Retirement Pool" situation
Retirement on a Shoestring (Howells), 188
retirement plans, 8, 186–87
rewards and challenges, as type
of meaning, 65
roadblocks, 22
in "Been There, Done That,
but Still Need to Earn"
situation, 89–93
in "Bored and Plateaued"
situation, 128–37
in "Bruised and Gun-shy"
situation, 108–17
to finding meaningful work,
67–80
age, 70
feeling that you can't
make a difference, 74–
75

FOR THE BEST IN PAPERBACKS, LOOK FOR THE

In every corner of the world, on every subject under the sun, Penguin represents quality and variety—the very best in publishing today.

For complete information about books available from Penguin—including Penguin Classics, Penguin Compass, and Puffins—and how to order them, write to us at the appropriate address below. Please note that for copyright reasons the selection of books varies from country to country.

In the United States: Please write to *Penguin Putnam Inc., P.O. Box 12289 Dept. B, Newark, New Jersey 07101-5289* or call 1-800-788-6262.

In the United Kingdom: Please write to *Dept. EP, Penguin Books Ltd, Bath Road, Harmondsworth, West Drayton, Middlesex UB7 0DA.*

In Canada: Please write to *Penguin Books Canada Ltd, 10 Alcorn Avenue, Suite 300, Toronto, Ontario M4V 3B2.*

In Australia: Please write to *Penguin Books Australia Ltd, P.O. Box 257, Ringwood, Victoria 3134.*

In New Zealand: Please write to *Penguin Books (NZ) Ltd, Private Bag 102902, North Shore Mail Centre, Auckland 10.*

In India: Please write to *Penguin Books India Pvt Ltd, 11 Panchsheel Shopping Centre, Panchsheel Park, New Delhi 110 017.*

In the Netherlands: Please write to *Penguin Books Netherlands bv, Postbus 3507, NL-1001 AH Amsterdam.*

In Germany: Please write to *Penguin Books Deutschland GmbH, Metzlerstrasse 26, 60594 Frankfurt am Main.*

In Spain: Please write to *Penguin Books S. A., Bravo Murillo 19, 1° B, 28015 Madrid.*

In Italy: Please write to *Penguin Italia s.r.l., Via Benedetto Croce 2, 20094 Corsico, Milano.*

In France: Please write to *Penguin France, Le Carré Wilson, 62 rue Benjamin Baillaud, 31500 Toulouse.*

In Japan: Please write to *Penguin Books Japan Ltd, Kaneko Building, 2-3-25 Koraku, Bunkyo-Ku, Tokyo 112.*

In South Africa: Please write to *Penguin Books South Africa (Pty) Ltd, Private Bag X14, Parkview, 2122 Johannesburg.*